PRAISE

"Years ago I was very lucky to be part of Charlie's team, it was the best team of the world and I personally experienced how the '7 steps' work.

Employees' loyalty, enthusiastic engagement, involvement, commitment and team work could be for a manager a dream difficult to achieve. The '7 steps' that Charlie provides in 'From OK to Excellence' will give to managers tools and techniques to make those dreams come true."

~ *Capt. Domenico Tringale, VP Port Operation at Carnival-Retired*

"The days of the employee who commits his or her life to one organization for 40 years or more are long gone. Employees in today's organizations are transient. Employee loyalty is earned, not mandated. It is very challenging to create a rewarding work environment, both financially and psychologically, that will garner employee involvement and commitment. Charlie Martin provides very grounded, down-to-earth tools for accomplishing something that many managers give up on too quickly…getting their employees to actively participate in the vision and success of the enterprise. If you run a company, a division, or a department, and want to truly enjoy your work, read this book. This is the book I wish I had years ago when I was cutting my teeth as a manager. These tools and techniques would have been very helpful, assuming I would have had the courage and resilience to use them."

~ *Guy Greco, Author of Mastering Strategy, co-Founder of Virtual CEO, Inc.*

Charlie's set of 7 imperatives for getting the most from your staff are valuable reminders of what excellent management requires. Interwoven within this clear message is a challenge to the reader to develop a personal plan using these same imperative tools. His advice to pause and really address the searching questions about personal values, goals, passions, and life direction is valuable and necessary. Charlie brings a wealth of personal experience to this excellent and practical guide for living a full life and successfully engaging others.

~ *James Dodwell, Senior Vice President Development,Capital Guidance Corporation*

"This book is a nuts and bolts look at all aspects of managing a business by someone who has walked the talk in all types and sizes of businesses. Unlike many books on the market, this is a practical "how to" book by someone who has learned by doing…not by guessing how things work in the real world."

~ *Kathy Fragnoli, J.D., President, The Resolution Group*

"I've had the good fortune to be a part of Charlie's team several times in the past 30 years. I can personally attest that if someone embraces and uses the tools Charlie has provided in From OK to Excellence, their work team will become more enthusiastically engaged, more pro-actively productive and more appreciative of the opportunity to work in such a great environment! The 7 steps work!"

~ *Ken Owens, VP Member and Owner Services, GetAways Resort Management*

"Charles Martin's no-nonsense, practical advice is presented clearly for every business manager to gain quick effective tools. His coaching style is refreshing."

~ *Graeme Gillies, Managing Director, Grayboy Entertainment*

"Charlie has helped us solve several specific problems over the past couple years. After reading his book, From OK to Excellence, we are now ready to apply much of what we have learned from the book to help us take our company to the next level."

~ *Paula Babin, President, Court Reporters Clearinghouse, Inc.*

"Relationships between employees and management are the most crucial elements in the success of any business. In today's ever changing world of increasing efficiency and doing things better, the management of staff and the creation of a happy and loyal workforce are the keys to success in any business environment. From OK to Excellence will provide a useful management tool."

~ *John Cleary, Chairman Australian Pharmacy Authority, Former Minister in Tasmanian Government, Former CEO Tiwi Islands*

FROM OK TO EXCELLENCE

7 Steps to a Productive Engaged Workforce

Charlie Martin

CPC PRESS

Copyright © 2015 Charlie Martin.

All Rights Reserved. No part of this book may be used or reproduced in any manner whatsoever without the written permission of the Publisher. Printed in the United States of America by CPC Press. For information address: 2315 Caringa Way, #48, Carlsbad, CA 92009.

Martin, Charlie. From OK to EXCELLENCE: The 7 Steps to a Productive, Engaged Workforce

Printed in the United States of America.

Acknowledgments

There are so many people who have contributed to the writing of this book that they are impossible to mention individually. Much of what has been included has been provided by various experiences throughout my long career driven by bosses, peers and team members as well as clients and their teams. I have learned from excellent bosses and team members and learned much about what not to do from bosses who were unable to provide the tools and guidance that would have been optimal. There are a few bosses and other executives that have been informal mentors for me and I will mention a few that clearly stand out. They are John Bland, Jack Ryan, Rocky Cox, Mike Feiner, Mark Anderson, George Miller, and Frank Clark.

I would like to acknowledge one additional person who made a very unknowing positive contribution to my growth and perspective and that is Frederick Herzberg one of the early workplace performance researchers. Attending a seminar led by Herzberg very early in my career stimulated what has become a lifelong interest in human behavior at work. That lifelong interest and study of human behavior at work has paid incredible dividends throughout my career.

Moving all of my experiences from rambling thoughts to readable usable information has been supported by many people. The support from my cover designer and layout facilitator Courtney Lawver of Pop X Graphics has been invaluable and very much appreciated. My editor Vicki Hogue has saved me from myself in terms of the correct usage of the English language. I am appreciative of the past clients, colleagues and others who have read the manuscript and provided comments representative of their early read and views of the manuscript and in many cases our past and current relationships.

I acknowledge the wonderful support from my wife Pia who always finds a way to give me incredible valuable feedback without putting our relationship at risk. Her input, support and help has been excellent and appreciated beyond words.

Contents

Introduction: _____ 1

An Overview from 5,000 Feet _____ 7

The Seven Steps _____ 19

    Step 1. Who are we, what do we do,
            where are we going? _____ 21

    Step 2. What's the plan? _____ 37

    Step 3. What do you want from me
            and where do I fit? _____ 49

    Step 4. How do I know how I am doing? _____ 59

    Step 5. What's in it for me … WIFM? _____ 65

    Step 6. Where are my tools? _____ 77

    Step 7. How do I learn, grow and progress? _____ 97

Summary, Review and Recommendations
for Leaders _____ 105

References and Resources _____ 117

FROM OK TO EXCELLENCE

7 STEPS TO A PRODUCTIVE ENGAGED WORKFORCE

Introduction:

Is OK Good Enough for YOU?

OK is that place where you're not failing and you're not succeeding. You're getting by. Is OK good enough when you experience it as a consumer? Is OK good enough if you or a loved one is having surgery? Is that where you want to be as a leader? Is that the tone you want to set for your workforce? Is getting by good enough? As a leader, whether you are the business owner, the department or division head or the front-line supervisor, your workforce is going to be the key to your success. You will set the tone and greatly influence their performance by your leadership and your standards.

Most annual reports declare, **"Our workforce is our most valuable asset."** Do daily actions of leaders toward the workforce support that declaration?

Is your workforce your biggest expense or your biggest asset? I don't believe you will find a workforce entry on your balance sheet, but you will clearly find payroll and related expenses on your income statement. How many of your discussions about your workforce are related to cutting costs versus investing in your most valuable asset? If your workforce is your biggest asset, even though it's not on your balance sheet, what and how much is it producing for you? How much time and energy are you spending on assuring that your workforce is as productive as it can be versus trying to reduce workforce costs? Are you getting the discretionary contribution from your workforce? Do they come to work and put in their time and do what they are told, or do they come to work to make a difference for you because of you?

This book will provide you with information that will help you see your workforce as your most valuable asset. You will also learn how you, as a leader, can help your workforce be as productive as possible. You'll gain the personal satisfaction of knowing that your leadership clearly makes a difference.

Workforce engagement levels in the United States have been stagnant at 30 percent for more than 15 years.

Since 2000, the Gallup Organization has conducted detailed research to determine the level of engagement of the workforce in the U.S. and around the world. In the U.S. the level of engagement has remained consistently around 30 percent, but has moved up to its highest level of 31.5 percent in the 2014 survey. This means that nearly 70 percent of the U.S. workforce is either not engaged or actively disengaged.

Another result from the 2014 Gallup survey may be even more frightening. The engagement of people categorized as manager, executive or officer is only 38.4 percent.

If less than 40 percent of those leading the charge are engaged, how can we expect more from our teams?

Another frightening survey result is related to the largest upcoming generation entering the workforce, the millennials. They will become the largest segment of the workforce and they are the least engaged group at 28.9 percent. In contrast, the traditionalists, most of whom have retired or will be soon, are at 42.2 percent.

If you are wondering about the level of engagement outside the U.S., it is even lower, at 13 percent.

So what's going on? Why have there been no meaningful gains in the Gallup workforce engagement surveys for 15 years?

There is no shortage of information about what motivates people to give their discretionary contribution at work, but still less than a third do.

The research ranges from work done by Abraham Maslow, Douglas McGregor, Fred Herzberg and others in the 1960's and 1970's to more current work done by Dan Pink in his recent book "Drive," Teresa Amabile and Steven Kramer in their recent book "The Progress Principle," "Flourish" by Martin Seligman, "Mindset" by Carol Dweck and others in between and since. All of these theories, along with additional well-researched management and leadership theories and tools, have not helped to move the needle.

In this book, I will provide an overview from 5,000 feet to demonstrate why moving the needle of workforce engagement beyond the stagnant less than one third is important to any business and to the U.S. economy in general. The financial benefits are huge.

The 7 Steps

Your workforce needs to know:

Step 1. Who you are, what you do and where you are going.
(Purpose, Mission, Vision and Values)

Step 2. What your plan is for getting there.
(Strategy and Corporate Goals)

Step 3. What you want from them and where they fit.
(Goal Setting and Alignment)

Step 4. How they will know how they are doing.
(Performance Feedback)

Step 5. What is in it for them?
(Recognition, Rewards, Appreciation and Feeling Successful)

Step 6. Where they will get the tools they need to do the job.
(Role of the Manager)

Step 7. How they will learn, grow and progress.
(Development Opportunities)

Leading teams or entire organizations is never an easy task. Challenges come from many directions. No two people are exactly alike. We complicate it more by our own challenge of trying to clearly understand who we are and why we have the beliefs we do.

When you look in the mirror, who do you see? Are you happy with the person looking back at you? Do you wonder what everybody else sees?

This book will provide you with **seven steps** to creating an engaged, productive workforce. More importantly, you will learn how to follow the **seven steps.**

In section one, you will get an overview of the level of workforce engagement in companies today. You will find more than enough reinforcement to support the steps you decide to take toward achieving the full engagement of your workforce. As you will see, the opportunities for improvement are staggering, and the possible positive bottom-line impacts are nearly overwhelming. One of the most important benefits of working toward the full engagement of your workforce is a highly satisfying, personal journey for you.

Imagine the personal satisfaction of creating a workplace where everyone is engaged and happy to be making a real difference every day. While you are imagining the future of the full engagement of your workforce, imagine the positive impact on your bottom-line profit, customer service, product quality, retention, absenteeism reduction, accident reduction and on and on. Everybody is a winner.

The **seven steps** will give you a template for creating and sustaining an engaged workforce. You will also find some interesting "bits and pieces" in each chapter that may be helpful in your own personal growth.

If you decide to follow the **seven steps** with enthusiasm, take the bits and pieces seriously and implement the ideas included, you will find that your workforce will be performing better than ever and that your life in general will be more enjoyable. Think about all the time you spend dealing with human resources issues. These so-called HR issues are generally driven by the failure to effectively implement one or more of the **seven steps.**

INTRODUCTION:

A famous coach once said, "Winning isn't everything, it's the only thing." Someone else said, "I don't care how much you know until I know how much you care."

My view is ... "If you get engaged yourself and follow the seven step template, you will not only see incredible and positive bottom-line results for your company, but you will also experience the personal satisfaction of knowing you have made an incredible and positive difference in the lives of the individual members of your workforce."

A Story by Moe

I want to introduce you to one of my clients, Moe. He is a small business owner, a great guy, he cares about his people, spends time communicating and no matter how much time he spends, he still finds that getting everyone on the same page, and staying there, is a big challenge. He has built a very successful business and it is still growing at a rate in excess of 20 percent per year at solid profit levels. As we worked together longer, Moe made a connection between his passion for his business and his passion for flying airplanes. Here is Moe's story:

> As Charlie my coach said, I have a passion for my business and a passion for flying. It wasn't until I started working with Charlie on how to better engage my team that I recognized the connection. It's not that everything that Charlie talks about relates to flying, it's the alignment of objectives that hit me as having a direct relationship. When I am at my business, I am the CEO, so I'm at the controls of the business. When I am flying, I am the CEO/captain of the airplane, unless I am not flying the left seat, at which time I'm in a supporting role. ... I'm usually the captain.
>
> One subtle difference between flying the plane and flying the business is that much of the alignment has already been handled by the manufacture of the airplane and its components. As the captain, it is my responsibility to understand which switches to move and what buttons to push at what time to cause the invisible team to work together. It's frightening for me to think about what would happen if all of those switches, wires, components and all of the related

electronic gear were not in alignment and instantly responsive to my command.

Granted I need to know what I am doing to fly the airplane safely, but I don't need to understand the detail of how all the systems work together to cause them to appropriately respond to my commands. I am able to push a button or move the stick and things just happen. As you might guess, since I don't have in-depth knowledge about how all of these systems work together, I assure that somebody who does understand all of that maintains the airplane for me to stringent aviation standards.

So, how does my flying relate to my business? I have now come to realize that if I want a safe, high-performing machine at my company, all of the people (the moving parts) must be aligned as well as all of those complex systems on my airplane. The difference is, the alignment I want in my business can't be pre-wired, it's reproduced multiple times each day by complex components called human beings. Although I may be able define what I want to get done and pass it on to the team, I have come to realize that it is extremely difficult to get the message across in the way I want it to come across on a consistent basis throughout my organization.

I am able to go the airplane instrument panel and flip a few switches and the team is aligned and ready to respond together to whatever I need done to achieve my goal. I have to spend much more time and energy if I want to achieve that same kind of response in my business. However, I have learned that the investment of my time on the front end produces great results and saves time on the back end.

I don't want to say too much more and take control of the message that Charlie wants you to receive. I would, however, like to emphasize that the objective is to get the same engagement and alignment and, therefore, focused responsiveness from my team that I get from my airplane. And I would like you to get that from your team. Charlie will be sharing with you his **seven steps** to creating and sustaining an engaged workforce, and I suggest that you take them seriously, understand them thoroughly and clearly and use them to your benefit.

Enjoy the journey.

Moe

An Overview from 5,000 Feet

There has been a great deal of research over the past few years about workforce engagement. Individual companies, large and small, are continually doing research. They continue to try to figure out how to get the highest performance from their workforces. Academic institutions do continual research to add to the body of knowledge. Behavioral scientists, in and out of academia, are always looking for a new twist. Statistics are gathered and sorted every way possible looking for answers. As a matter of fact, there have been many conclusions drawn about possible answers.

Bottom line, the percent of the U.S. workforce that is fully engaged has not noticeably moved in 15 years.

In an August 2015 article, Jim Clifton of Gallup announced that Gallup and McKinsey, both leaders in their respective areas, had formed the Organizational Science Initiative. The stated purpose of this new organization is to create the most comprehensive analytics ever on the subject of behavioral economics for organizations, or more simply, the role human nature plays in virtually all organizational outcomes.

The article goes on to say that although it may sound simplistic, Gallup's conclusion is that a global economic turnaround will be driven by 10 million leaders around the world running their organizations not just better, but differently. Organizations everywhere have already made process improvements through initiatives such as Six Sigma and lean management. They are already "leaner and meaner." What they haven't done is master the engagement of their workforces.

McKinsey's research shows that the healthiest organizations generate nearly three times the returns of less healthy companies, which means that companies are leaving hundreds of millions or billions of dollars on the table.

In the article, Clifton stated that "Global GDP is running out of gas. This means that the world's citizens aren't making and trading enough to support population growth, food and shelter needs, infrastructure development, the creation of good jobs, adequate healthcare, and so on. Global well-being is running out of gas, too. Our mission is to fix these problems and help get the global economy back on track."

What Is Engagement?

My definition of full engagement goes something like this:

Full engagement (at work or in life in general) is waking up every morning with a positive focus. It is opening your eyes and seeing possibilities, seeing all the good things about whatever you are doing, seeing the glass half full or perhaps completely full, looking for challenges and opportunities, not problems.

Whether you are going to a job, or you own a business, it is going there with the objective of doing your very best job supporting the company and looking for opportunities for improvement. Full engagement is:

- Helping your boss or subordinates be successful
- Supporting your co-workers
- Making positive comments as opposed to negative ones
- Giving your discretionary effort
- Sharing your ideas
- Coming to work every day and on time
- Being inquisitive and curious
- Always wanting to know more
- Asking thoughtful questions
- Continually learning
- Looking for more responsibility, or at least a way to contribute more
- Living in the moment, not in tomorrow or yesterday

The variance between this definition and a definition of non-engaged or actively disengaged is vast. Negative engagement in my view would be spending all of your time doing the opposite of all of the things outlined under full engagement, and trying to make sure nobody else has the ability to be fully engaged due to your actions.

Somewhere between the fully engaged and the actively disengaged rests most of the working population.

A great deal of research about workforce behavior has been conducted by the Gallup Organization. Since they finalized their questions in the late 90s, their survey has been administered to more than 25 million employees in 195 different countries in 70 languages. They chose to break engagement into three categories: engaged, not engaged and actively disengaged. Their definitions are as follows:

"Engaged employees work with passion and feel a profound connection to their company. They drive innovation and move the organization forward."

"Not-engaged employees are essentially 'checked out.' They're sleepwalking through their workday, putting in time—but not energy or passion—into their work."

"Actively disengaged employees aren't just unhappy at work, they're busy acting out their unhappiness. Every day, these workers undermine what their engaged co-workers accomplish."

In October 2000, Gallup provided their first report on the "engaged," "not engaged" and "actively disengaged" in the U.S. economy. The national trend indicated that less than a third of the workforce in the United States was engaged while approximately a fifth was actively disengaged. These statistics have been updated quarterly since then.

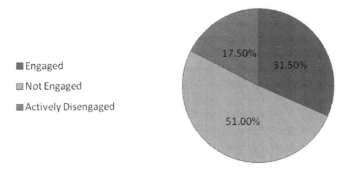

2014 Employee Engagement Levels

These statistics have a very significant financial impact. The Gallup Organization has calculated the cost to the U.S. economy of actively disengaged employees is over $500 billion annually.

The Gallup research goes on to say that a conservative estimate of the loss of productivity of an actively disengaged employee is $3,400 per $10,000 of annual salary. For example, if an employee earns $30,000, the cost is $10,200 and you can do the math as the salary goes up.

There is a little good news if your workforce is small (if you call a 33-percent engagement level good news). In companies with 50 or fewer employees, the engagement level is 33 percent and the actively disengaged level is 12 percent. The numbers get a bit less friendly as the size of the workforce goes up. The level of engagement for an employee base of 10,000-plus is 22 percent, while the actively disengaged grows to 19 percent.

This level of engagement and disengagement for smaller groups is primarily driven by the greater sense of local control and the feeling of connection to and accountability for company output.

It is clear that in work units of fewer than 10, the engagement level will soar or plummet depending on the owner/leader/manager.

You may also be thinking or wondering about the impact of workforce age on engagement. Again, according to the most recent research by Gallup, there are some differences in engagement between age-based work groups.

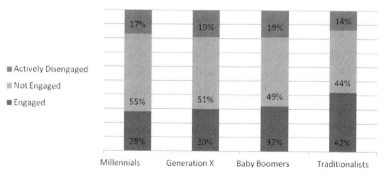

Corporate Executive Board Engagement Levels

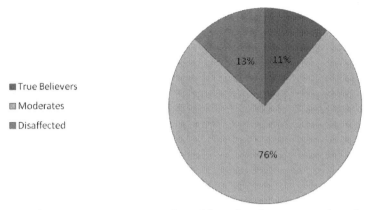

The Corporate Executive Board has also done research and provided similar, but slightly different, statistics.

A wide range of areas are impacted by not engaged or actively disengaged employees.

Employee accidents cost employers billions of dollars each year, while also, of course, causing pain and suffering to the injured and impacting those people around them.

Absenteeism costs billions each year. Gallup reported that actively disengaged employees miss in excess of four more workdays per year.

Customer service is significantly impacted by the engagement level of the workforce. Oftentimes the least engaged employees are directly dealing with your customers.

Turnover is a huge cost in some industries and a large concern to any company. One study pegged the cost of turnover for U.S. companies at $3 trillion. Even if that statistic is 50-percent wrong, the numbers are still staggering.

The statistics published by the Corporate Leadership Council of the Corporate Executive Board show that the costs of turnover are extremely high, from the bottom to the top of organizations.

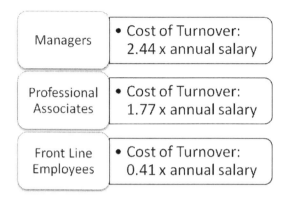

Other research organizations have found in recent studies that about one third of the millions of employees they surveyed recently plan to resign within two years. They also say that turnover is predictable. Past surveys show that 64 percent of those employees who answered "not sure," or "no," to survey questions about their intent to leave within two years, actually left within five years.

It doesn't take long to apply these findings to your turnover at each level to see your cost-saving opportunity just in this one area.

The Corporate Executive Board also studied the relationship between engagement, discretionary effort and retention. The survey included more than 50,000 employees in 59 organizations across the globe. The results indicated that increased engagement can result in up to a 57-percent increase in discretionary effort and up to an 87-percent reduction in desire to leave the organization.

How valuable would a 57-percent productivity improvement be for your company? How about a big improvement in your retention rate? What are you doing about it? More on this topic later, we're still at 5,000 feet looking at the landscape.

There is also the issue of well-being, which leads to absenteeism and performance issues. Gallup has done significant research in this area and found that engaged workers lead healthier lives. Gallup defined well-being as all the things that affect how people think about and experience their lives. The statistics cited below are supported by the findings of the extensive Gallup research.

Gallup found that employees who are engaged are generally healthier and have healthier habits than those who are not engaged or who are actively disengaged. Engaged employees tend to have fewer health challenges and are more often in the safe zone for disease factors such as high blood pressure, high cholesterol, diabetes, diagnosed depression and heart attacks. Employees who are engaged also tend to eat healthier diets and exercise more frequently than their actively disengaged co-workers.

Gallup categorized well-being levels in three categories.

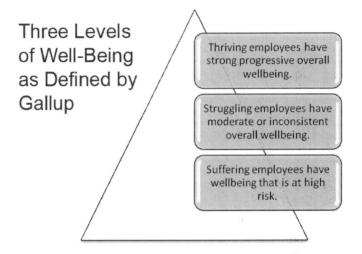

When employees are engaged and thriving, and both their workplace and personal lives are running smoothly, disruptions in their personal or work lives are unlikely to throw them off course. These people are physically healthy, have strong relationships, are active in their communities and have their personal finances under control.

These factors add up to employees who are more productive, are at work more often and are more likely to stay with their present employers. They tend to have 46-percent fewer unhealthy days as a result of physical or mental illness, are 39-percent less likely to be diagnosed with a new disease in the next year and are 43-percent less likely to be diagnosed with anxiety or depression.

You may be getting the feeling that the engagement or lack of engagement in your workforce can have a dramatic impact on the success of your business and perhaps on your personal performance as well.

Is engagement about passion or commitment or focus or what? The answer may be some combination of all those factors.

Passion, What Is It?

Let's talk about passion. What is passion anyway?

Look it up on Wikipedia or read the entry in a standard hard-copy dictionary and you can get a crisp definition. Conversations about passion have been around for a long time. As a trained coach, I am always engaging in conversations about passion. It seems that everyone wants to be passionate about something, and most of us probably are. The question is, how many of us are passionate about something related to work? My experience and the statistics about engagement would infer not nearly enough.

As a manager with years of experience in a variety of environments, I am always interested to learn that just because someone who works in my organization doesn't seem to be passionate about his or her job, it doesn't necessarily mean they aren't wildly passionate about something else.

I have learned that front-line employees, as well as managers, who don't seem to be engaged at work have many other pursuits outside of their jobs. Many employees are mayors or councilpersons in their communities, serve on local school boards or are PTA presidents, are on the boards of their homeowners associations and so on. These people spend a great many more hours at work than they do in these other activities. Why haven't we been able to engage them at work? Is it possible they are just tuned out at work and have given up on engagement or passion? We are getting small pieces of their capability and none of their discretionary energy. Who is responsible?

Is it possible to find passion at work? As leaders and managers, what can we do to support people finding their passion at work, or perhaps us finding ours? The answer is complex because people are complex. We are not going to provide a cookie cutter answer in this book that will create instant passion in every person in the workforce. I will provide the **seven steps** which, if effectively followed, will clearly improve the level of engagement.

The real secret for you as a business owner/manager/ leader is to be engaged enough yourself that you become engaged with each person on your team.

Get to know them individually with the honest intention of helping them find their passion and provide them with the opportunity to fully engage at work.

The ongoing concern and conversation about how to get the most from your workforce is not new. What is new is the research done in the past few years around the topic of workforce engagement, and how to maximize it. There is no shortage of viewpoints. I have uncovered just the tip of the iceberg of what some of the research is saying about engagement and what the value might be to companies. As we get into the heart of the book, I will provide information about what it takes to move the needle of workforce engagement in a positive direction.

I am hopeful that the information presented in this overview has been sufficiently compelling to cause you to want to learn more. The thing I haven't addressed is what does this mean from an emotional standpoint and what might it mean to you personally?

Are you personally fully engaged with life? Is being a business owner or executive right for you? Are you in the right job or career field doing what you were meant to do? Are you doing what you are passionate about? If your answers are yes, you must be at the top of your game. Congratulations.

You will be able to use the information presented in the rest of the book to maximize the performance of your workforce. I suggest that by using the information presented here to generate more engagement from your workforce you will get good results and personal satisfaction as well. You may want to take some time to think about what you're up to. Use the guidelines presented here to have a good look at how you can become fully engaged. The steps presented here are related to achieving results through others, but the concept and the steps are the same for you personally.

At the end of each chapter, I will provide insight on how you can maximize your personal engagement as well.

Conversations from engaged teams have a uniquely positive tone, let's listen in.

Imagine it's another Monday morning and you, a hard-working leader, manager, business owner or executive, show up at work. What kind of a day do you think it's going to be?

Imagine today is your normal kind of day. When you arrive, your team is present and busy. Not only are they all there and hard at work, but they also seem happy and fully engaged in making a difference for themselves, the customers and for you.

Since we are imagining, let's drop in on some conversations, unobserved of course.

Three employees talking while taking a break:

Bob: "Can you believe what a difference we make in the lives of our customers?"

Sue: "Yea, it feels good to be part of a company that really encourages us to make a difference for our customers, instead of just trying to make a buck. It was never like this at the other company I worked for. I never knew why we were doing what we did or what impact it had on anything. I felt like I was just there to get a paycheck and I didn't really care that much about how the company was doing. I can't even begin to explain how much different I feel working here."

Sean: "Yea, I never really understood why I felt different here until Joe became our boss. He has really opened my eyes. I feel totally different now. Somehow I feel like I make a difference, and I like it."

Three senior executives talking:

Al: "I think everyone on the team understands the strategy now, what do you think?"

Sharon: "I agree. The feedback I received from the rest of the team has been good. They said that when the strategy was discussed throughout the company, there was a healthy discussion, quite a few intelligent questions, and a solid consensus at the end. The challenge now is to be able to create the same level of clarity about our goals."

Shannon: "Yea, it's key for everybody to understand how to set their goals and how they tie into the company goals. It's absolutely certain that if the team isn't clear about where we are going, there's no telling where we might end up. Let's not start a trip without a map."

Al: "This year we need to do a better job of making sure everybody knows where we are going and where they fit as well."

If you are part of a team and you don't know what the goal is or what part you play in achieving it, why show up?

The conversation between the three senior executives continues....

Shannon: "We need to be sure that everyone understands how we measure success in every area this year."

Sharon: "Right, it's been a bit painful this past year. It seemed like we had a different set of numbers for everything and none of them matched. It's no wonder we didn't make our goals, we never really knew how we were doing until it was too late to do anything about it."

Al: "After our strategy meeting and team agreement, I believe this year is going to be really different and much better."

A group of employees talking in the break room:

Andy: "Does anybody understand this new incentive program that was introduced last week? It isn't clear to me. I'm happy with my salary and benefits, but I don't understand this new thing."

Charlie: "I understand it. Andy, while you were out last week Barbara held meetings with us and explained everything. We had lots of input and a good discussion with everyone tossing in their two cents worth. It was great."

Bonnie: "I know Barbara is out today, but I'll bet she will be meeting with you personally when she gets back to be sure you understand how the new incentive program works and how it will affect you."

Andy: "I really like being included on the things that affect me."

A manager talking with the Human Resources manager:

Ken: "We have a new analyst starting next week. I have arranged for her office and all of her technology support equipment to be ready. Do you have all of the paperwork she will need to complete ready to go? Is she scheduled for orientation, is someone meeting her when she arrives and has a mentor been selected? I want to be sure that she gets off to a good start. Let me know if there is anything else I can do to make sure that she is comfortable from the beginning."

Clara: "I know, Ken, and I certainly agree with you; it was hard enough to find someone of her caliber and I sure want her to know she has joined a great team and how happy we are to have her. I've got you covered.

With these and other similar conversations going on around the company, is it any wonder that the workforce is at work, on time and engaged?

Although we didn't see all of them at play in the conversations above, the implementation of the **seven steps** throughout any organization will create these kinds of positive conversations. As you progress through the book, you will learn more about the **seven steps** and how to use them in your company to achieve sensational results.

The Seven Steps

I have found that as I work with companies to help them achieve maximum engagement from their workforces, it is an easy conversation to have, but is a little harder to actually do. It requires positive intent on the part of leadership as well as good planning, clear communication, involvement, focus and discipline. And no steps can be skipped.

If you decide to take action as a result of reading this book, take time to think about what you really want to achieve and take time to prepare. Most important is your commitment to start and finish the implementation of these **seven steps** and then continue to use them. As your business and your life changes you will need to tweak some of the details in the steps but the fundamentals will never change. Once you start you are in it forever, if you want to sustain an engaged workforce.

The remainder of this book will provide you with information that, when appropriately applied, will make a big difference for you and will drive an enormous return on your time investment.

If you have read this far, you more than likely understand that improving the level of engagement of your workforce will pay solid dividends. I suggest, if you want to have maximum success with this book that you take the approach outlined in the box:

Suggestions for Getting the Most from this Book

1. Read the book front to back one time; it will be a quick and easy read.

2. Read it again, taking the time to identify each point as it is discussed, especially those that are not in place in your organization. Make detailed notes so you are clear about what is really missing.

3. Make notes on what you would like to do about the things that are missing, what you actually need to do to correct them, and who you need to help you.

4. Develop a plan for how you will proceed, including details of how you will engage whoever you need to help you along the way.

5. Get started.

STEP 1.

WHO ARE WE, WHAT DO WE DO, WHERE ARE WE GOING?

Purpose, Values, Mission and Vision

Yes, the title of Step 1 is a mouthful. However, these topics together form the core of what all businesses are about, something that the workforce can relate to and sign up for. We will discuss each of these topics.

Purpose

The word purpose is very popular at the moment, as it should be. Without having a purpose that is larger than ourselves, it is difficult for any of us to have the drive (intrinsic motivation) to achieve what we are meant to be, or to self-actualize. As business owners, one of the most critical things we can do is determine what the purpose of our businesses are beyond making a few bucks. In most cases, there is more to what we are trying to do with our businesses than just accumulating wealth. The purpose is often a combination of the values, mission and vision, and paints a picture of possibilities that can create motivation for the workforce.

Values

Does every organization have values? If you took a wide-ranging survey, no matter how organizations answer the question, they do have values. I asked a few members of a client's management team a related question. "What are the things that you always do or never do at your company?" I got answers all over the place but no particular clarity around the answers to the question. I was really asking a values question, without naming it that. Later, through more in-depth conversations, I learned that this company did have values, and they were written out, but they clearly were not at the top of everyone's minds and they were not being lived by everyone.

Do you think it's important to have values that are thought through and clear to everyone in your organization? I hope you do, because it is important. Your organization values determine, or at least should determine, the behavior of everyone in the organization, starting with you. If you don't proactively clarify your organizational values, what do you think will happen? The answer is clear: The individual people in your organization will bring the values they have and apply them at your organization. How could they be expected to do anything else? If everyone has the same values that you do, perhaps this will work out fine. If not, perhaps it will not work out so well. Hopefully, you agree with the need for values and if you do, they are in place in your organization and being lived every day.

What if you don't have values in place? How do you go about developing your values?

There are plenty of methods for creating your values. Before you go down the path of creating values, you need to think through why you are doing it and what you expect as the result. If creating values is something you want to do on your own, expecting everyone to follow those values may be OK if you are a startup and the initial values only apply to you. If your company has been around for a while and you don't have clear, published values, then I suggest a different approach.

There is plenty of research to suggest that the things people are involved in creating become theirs. People are more likely to follow and live by values they helped create than if they are provided by someone else. It will be worth your time to engage other people in the development of your company values. You might ask how many other people should be engaged. How many do you want to understand, believe in and follow whatever values are created? If you have an extremely large group, it will be impossible to involve everyone but you can certainly put together a representative group from each segment of your company.

I suggest that before you involve anyone in the development of your company values, or even mention it, that you clarify what your personal values are. It is unlikely that you will want the values that are important to your organization to conflict with your personal values. Start by writing a paragraph or more about what your organization would feel like if it was living all of your values. Once you complete this step, convert that feeling into a set of core value statements. Keep them to yourself for now.

Perhaps you have words like integrity, fairness, respect, and so on, as values. Once you have progressed to this level, it is time to decide to what degree you will engage your organization in the process. It may feel like you already have values in mind and could as easily put some phrases around your key value words and be done with it. You may also feel that it is a bit less than transparent to have clarified your own values and still be asking your team to create the organizational values with you. The reality is, unless you have a rather unusual workforce, they are likely to come up with a set of core values similar to your own. And, since they will have participated, they will own them along with you. If your team's input doesn't exactly match yours, you can probably get to the right final solution with a good discussion and some tweaking.

The best way to get everyone engaged in this process is to ask them to use the same process you just did, with a twist. Draft a memo to the entire organization, or hold a meeting if your group is small enough, explaining what you are trying to do and why. Let them know that they will be meeting with you to discuss how the process will work, and assure them that you want and need their involvement. If you have a management team, ask them to meet with the appropriate size groups to discuss the values project in more detail. The process should be identical throughout the organization.

Ask each employee to write his or her feelings about how the organization will feel with the appropriate values in place. Then ask them to convert their feelings into a few key value words. Once everyone has completed this step, have them meet in small groups or all together if your organization is small enough, to reach an agreement on the key words that represent their true values. Don't limit the number of words. Also, tell them that the end process will result in a values statement that will be published throughout the organization.

You can boil all the input down into solid value statements that truly represent the views of the entire organization, one that also supports your values. When you have a final document, take time to thank everyone for their input and introduce the new values, with as many face-to-face meetings as necessary. This will take time, but the investment will be worth it.

We will be talking about mission and vision as we continue. Much of the communication process will be similar. You may decide that if you are going to be doing the values, mission, and vision you may want to introduce them as a group; it depends on the ability of your workforce to assimilate information, and how much time you are able to spend on this project.

Mission Statement

What is a mission statement anyway and do you really need one? The decision on whether you need one is up to you. Before you make that decision, I have a very short story for you.

There was a woman, a traveling business executive, walking down a street in a major city in the world. Alongside the road there were three stonecutters working. The traveling business executive asked the first worker what he was doing. "I'm carving a piece of stone," he said. "That's what my boss told me to do." She asked the same question of the second person. "I'm building a wall," she said. Again, she posed the same question to the third person. "I'm creating a cathedral," he replied.

What is your cathedral?

Does your workforce know what your cathedral is? The idea of having a mission statement has been around a very long time and there are many different viewpoints on what it's really about and what it means. I like to think of a mission statement as a statement that clearly defines an organization's reason for being. If done well, it should be the basis for the organization's plans and goals. It is the answer to the questions: Why are we in business? Who are we serving? Why are we the way we are? What are we trying to accomplish? The mission should be something that everybody who is part of the organization or deals with the organization can understand and use to evaluate the success of the organization. It is your company's cathedral.

You might wonder how long a mission statement should be. Only you can answer that. It needs to be long enough to ensure the intended message gets across to all of the intended audiences. Who the intended audiences are is also up to you. Companies call their mission statement many different things and start the statement with keywords like, at XYZ Company we believe, or the XYZ Way, etc. At the end of the day, it doesn't matter what you call it as long as it represents the best thinking of all appropriate people in the organization and represents what the company does. It's also good if the statement is easy to remember so all stakeholders can easily recall it in casual conversations.

Some organizations have been able to create a persona as a mission statement. Tommy Bahama, the clothing brand, took that approach, and from all outside appearances has made it work. While working on a project with them I learned that all key decisions at Tommy Bahama are made after asking the question, "What would Tommy do?" There is no Tommy, but they have developed a persona around a lifestyle that drives their decision making. It is who they are and the Tommy persona drives how they act and how they treat each other and impacts what items they carry in their stores and restaurants. I have had significant exposure to the senior management team of Tommy Bahama, and can verify that they spend a good deal of time assuring they are always doing what Tommy would do.

The time spent considering what your mission really is will be worth it, particularly if you want to achieve maximum engagement from your workforce. I'm not sure that mission statements about maximizing shareholder value or achieving some profit target, for example, are likely to drive engagement or help define your purpose. I'm not sure mission statements with those things as a prominent feature are really about building a cathedral. Try to think about the emotional engagement of your team, as well as your own emotional connection, when you start working on your mission statement.

Ask yourself if the mission statement you create is going to serve as a tool to allow you to maximize the performance and relationships with all your intended audiences. After thinking it through, put together the right combination of people and give it a shot.

There are a variety of methods you can employ when creating your mission statement. As you will recall from our earlier discussion about creating your values, I am a big advocate of involving as many people as you can in the process to create joint ownership. I would suggest that, at a minimum, you fully engage your senior management team in the process. If the senior team is small and the next level of management, if you have one, is small as well, you will add value by including them.

Most of my experience in helping organizations develop mission statements has been with the owner directly or the owner and senior leadership team. My role has been to act as coach and facilitator to help them establish clarity about what business they are really in and how to convert that to a mission statement. It is likely that the development of your mission or vision statement will be aided by using an outside facilitator to keep the energy flowing while you work toward creating your best result.

A few years ago, I was a senior member of the management team for a quarter-billion-dollar company that found itself needing to reposition. In this case, a complete repositioning of the brand included a new logo and all the related materials along with a new marketing focus. There is no way we could have accomplished the necessary work and achieved the objectives of the repositioning without an outside resource. This entire process had to start with redefining who we were and how we wanted to be viewed by all our different audiences. In other words, we needed to redefine our mission which would impact a number of other things.

The mission statement process will require more strategic and creative thinking than the value creation process. You will need to think through what you currently do, what is at the core of your business, who are your customers, what market segment are you in and more. In fact, you may not have ever clearly defined what business you are in and this will be a good time to do that. You may find this process more difficult than you think. You may also find that in the process of clarifying what business you're in, it is not the business you thought you were in, or intended to be in. I'm not suggesting that you don't know what you are doing. What I am suggesting is that your core business may have gradually changed over time and you may not have had time to notice the gradual shifts. The best way to proceed is to get your senior management team together and start talking about what you're up to. Ask yourself the hard questions. Some good questions are outlined in the box on the next page.

These questions are just a good start and most are not particularly easy to answer without solid thinking. Don't stop with these questions. Make this a rigorous process; it will pay dividends. We will discuss some similar questions when we talk about vision.

The process of developing your mission statement should not be rushed. Get it right so you don't find yourself doing it again in the near future. One of the major benefits of getting it right is that you can use it long enough and consistently over a period of time that it becomes ingrained in all of your audiences. It will clearly become who you are. I suggest that you don't try to do it all in one session. It will be useful for you and your team to let the work you have done rest for a few days and then come back to it fresh with additional thoughts in future discussions.

Once you and your senior team think you have it right, you should find a way to engage the rest of the organization in giving you feedback about whether it makes sense to them. This can be done in a variety of ways, but however you decide to do it, do not give the rest of the team the impression that it is a done deal and you are just looking for a sign off. You should want as much candid input as you can get. Chances are good that if you have done a good job, the rest of the workforce will not have any major issues with what you have created. However you decide to get additional input from the rest of the organization, the more personal you get the better. The same comments that were made earlier about communicating the finished product apply here as well.

Questions to Aid in Defining Your Mission

- What are the core drivers of your success?
- Who are your most important customers?
- What are you better at than your competition?
- Who is your competition?
- What are you known for?
- Are you in the same business you were in two years ago? Will you be in the same business five years from now?
- What do you really do?
- What makes you different?

Sample Mission Statements

Nike Mission Statement
To bring inspiration and innovation to every athlete* in the world.
*"If you have a body, you are an athlete."

Amazon Mission Statement
Our vision is to be earth's most customer centric company; to build a place where people can come to find and discover anything they might want to buy online.

Walt Disney Mission Statement
To make people happy.

Walmart Mission Statement
To give ordinary folk the chance to buy the same thing as rich people.

Apple Mission Statement
Apple is committed to bringing the best personal computing experience to students, educators, creative professionals and consumers around the world through its innovative hardware, software and Internet offerings.

Coca Cola Mission Statement
To refresh the world… To inspire moments of optimism and happiness… To create value and make a difference.

Microsoft Mission Statement
Microsoft's mission is to enable people and businesses throughout the world to realize their full potential.

McDonald's Mission Statement
McDonald's brand mission is to be our customers' favorite place and way to eat.

Facebook Mission Statement
Facebook's mission is to give people the power to share and make the world more open and connected.

Google Mission Statement
Google's mission is to organize the world's information and make it universally accessible and useful.

Vision

You may be wondering what the difference is between mission and vision. The mission, as we mentioned earlier, is what you are doing. It is your purpose, reason for being, something to be accomplished. The vision, on the other hand, is what you want to become, something to be pursued. The vision is the word picture of what your organization will be at some future time and sets the direction for what you strive to become. Many times you will see vision statements say something like "be the best" or "become the biggest." You will find that the best or biggest is hard to measure. That doesn't mean you shouldn't strive to be the biggest or best, it's just hard to tell when you have arrived and it doesn't necessarily tickle the emotional heartstrings.

Here are a few vision statements that I have come across.

Nike
1960's: Crush Adidas.
Current: To be the number one athletic company in the world.

IKEA
The IKEA vision is to create a better everyday life for many people. We make this possible by offering a wide range of well-designed, functional home furnishing products at prices so low that as many people as possible will be able to afford them.

Ken Blanchard Companies
To be the number one advocate in the world for human worth in organizations.

Honda
1970: We will destroy Yamaha.
Current: To be the company that our shareholders and society want.

Sony
1950's: Become the Company most known for changing the worldwide poor-quality image of Japanese products.
Current: Sony is a leading manufacturer of audio, video, communications and information technology products for the consumer and professional markets. Its motion picture, television, computer entertainment, music and online businesses make Sony one of the most comprehensive entertainment companies in the world.

Qualcomm
To deliver the world's most innovative wireless solutions.

Zappos
One day, 30% of all retail transactions in the US will be online. People will buy from the company with the best service and the best selection. Our hope is that our focus on service will allow us to WOW our customers, our employees, our vendors, and out investors. We

want Zappos.com to be known as a service company that happens to sell shoes, handbags, and anything and everything.

Avon Products
To be the company that best understands the products and services that support the self-fulfillment of women-globally.

I could go on, and I have no comments to make about any of the vision statements above. The point is they are all different.

When you begin work on a vision statement it's important to remember that the vision is about who or what you want to become. In many regards what you want to become may be more compelling to your various audiences than what you are today. On the other hand, many companies combine the mission and vision into a statement of purpose or some sort of credo. Much like the process of creating your values and mission statement it will be important that you give the process of creating your vision statement serious thought. Think about where you are headed and what you want to become as an organization. The vision statement can energize your entire organization if it is exciting and even a little intimidating, while still achievable.

The process of developing your vision statement is similar to the development of your mission statement; however, I recommend that your vision statement is more appropriately developed by the senior team. The senior team will, in most cases, be in a better position to understand the possibilities and constraints of an uncertain future, and they can balance a stretch vision with the right amount of reality. It is, however, unlikely that you will cause any damage by discussing possibilities with a wider audience. The risk you take is raising expectations and then being unable or unwilling to accept the input.

You should now have a better understanding of purpose, a clear grasp of the relationship between values, mission and vision, and have some ideas about how to put them together. The point of this book is to provide the **seven steps** to an engaged workforce. Purpose, values, mission and vision are valuable tools in the creation of full engagement. If done correctly, they are at the core of defining your cathedral, so when the person on the street asks one of your people what they are doing, they can provide your equivalent of building a cathedral.

Let's assume that you have values in place, a mission and a vision statement or some combination, and they clearly define your purpose.

Let's also assume that you have engaged everyone possible in the development of these statements. Now what?

The involvement steps you have taken will be valuable in the further engagement of your workforce.

Starting now, and for the rest of the time you own the business, or are a key leader in this organization, it's all about communicating and living the values and conducting business in a manner that is driven by the purpose/mission/vision and values. The communication of the purpose, mission, vision, values is vital to success.

Communicating the values is probably the easiest. In most cases, the values are very fundamental principles that have been adopted by the organization. Hopefully they have been jointly developed and the entire organization knows what they are and agrees with them. Even if this is the case, it will still be important to hold meetings with the entire workforce to reinforce that the values belong to everyone and were developed with the input of everyone. These meetings should be conducted by the business owner or other leaders at the highest level that is reasonable. The message to be delivered is that these values belong to the entire organization and that everyone will be held accountable for living them every day. The values will drive the behavior of the people in the organization from top to bottom.

The values must be published in employee manuals, included in orientations and kept as visible as possible forever so that nobody has any doubt about what the shared values of the organization are. It must become obvious over time that the entire organization is actually living by the values. It will destroy trust immediately if anyone in the organization, particularly a member of the leadership team, is allowed to violate one of the values without appropriate action being taken. I can not stress enough the importance of living the values.

The communication of the mission and vision may be more challenging. Even though there may have been plenty of involvement by as many people as possible in the development of the mission and vision the communication of them will still be a challenge.

I will share with you the process used by one of my clients. This client is in the restaurant business with two brands, 13 locations and about 700 employees spread over four states.

The managing partner and I agreed at the beginning of our relationship that he needed to develop both mission and vision statements. We arrived at that decision after a discussion of what he was really trying to accomplish with his business and what his related personal objectives were. I have found that in many cases the objectives outlined by my clients get back to the need to answer two key questions. What are they really trying to achieve, and why are they trying to achieve it? The answers to these and related questions nearly always leads back to the desire and need for the full engagement of their workforce from top to bottom.

Based on the discussions with this client we agreed to start with the development of the mission and vision statements. I will discuss the first phase, the development and initial communication of the mission and vision statements.

Here is what we did:

We, the owners and I, met with the senior management team made up of the regional directors and the director of administration. We began a discussion about what mission and vision statements are all about and the potential value they can add. It didn't take long for the team to understand the value of both and start discussing possibilities. I have found that in many cases the discussion about these topics takes a great deal of time. In this case we were able to get to an agreed mission statement in very short order. The vision statement took a bit more time and was ultimately finalized after more discussion over a period of time.

The mission statement that was arrived at by this management team is outstanding. It is: "To make lifetime friends by creating a special feeling for our team, our guests and our vendors." Understanding that the next step in this process is communicating the message, this particular mission statement has great legs. It provides opportunities for communicating clearly with all key stakeholders, the customers, the employees and the companies that supply all the goods and services the company relies on.

As we discuss the rest of the roll out of the **seven steps** for an engaged workforce you will see how this mission statement aids in the process.

After getting total agreement on the mission statement with the senior team we needed to decide how to roll it out to the rest of the organization. Considering the geographical dispersion of this company, the decision was made that the senior team would go back and meet with all of the general managers of the locations. This process would give them the opportunity to explain the mission statement and how we developed it. The GM's were then asked to share the mission statement in personal meetings with all of the employees at each location.

Since, in the restaurant business, there are full- and part-time employees working on a wide variety of shifts, this process took a few days, but the message was shared with all employees. In addition, a variety of other actions were taken. Employee surveys were developed and implemented to begin to learn how the employees feel they are being treated and to determine if they are having that special feeling. The mission statement is being incorporated into all new hire orientation material and all vendors have been contacted to let them know how important they are and that they are a key part of the company's mission. The company is making changes to customer-facing materials to include the mission statement wherever possible and reasonable. Customer comment cards are being changed to ask customers to describe that special feeling they get when dining in one of the restaurants. Large boards, featuring the mission statement in the company colors and the company logo, have been constructed; the boards are mounted in prominent locations in work areas for all employees to see continually.

In addition to all the things described above, this mission statement lends itself perfectly to the establishment of clear goals for every employee in the company. We will talk more about that process as we move forward.

The vision that was established for this company is equally compelling and clear. At the time of the writing of this book, it had not been as fully communicated as the mission statement, however. The process of communicating the vision will be similar but will not be as intense. The vision does not engage anyone beyond the employee group, so the communication will be focused on the management team and the employee group. Every employee will know the vision and how it relates to them. They will receive personal communication much like they did for the mission. The vision will be visible on internal documents and will be used to encourage employees, at all levels, to look at future possibilities for themselves within the company. Once again, the vision can be used to drive performance through goal clarification.

We will come back to this later as we discuss goal setting.

Now some bits and pieces for you

As you think about your life, have you solidified your purpose, established your values, clarified your mission and defined you vision? What do you stand for? Who are you, where are you going, and why are you going there? Think about these questions thoroughly. What is your purpose? As you make key decisions in your life, having a clear picture of who you are and why you are the way you are will add big value. It will provide a life template that you can use to weigh decisions. Think about this: You are wearing a very different pair of glasses than anyone else. There is nobody that you know that has the exact experience and characteristics that you do. Think of the impact of a few of the things in the box on the way you see life and behave.

> **These factors and more define your special pair of glasses:**
>
> - Who your parents are
> - Where you were born
> - Where you grew up
> - Where you went to school (elementary, high school, college, etc.)
> - Your age
> - Where you have lived
> - Your sex
> - Your nationality
> - Where you have worked
> - Your religious preference
> - Your marital status
> - Your parental status or not
> - So on and so on

The point of this is that there is nobody exactly like you, so no other person's reality is going to be exactly the same as yours. You have designed and will continue to solidify your personal filters. How could anyone else see the world exactly as you do? Think about it, when decision time comes, it goes something like this:

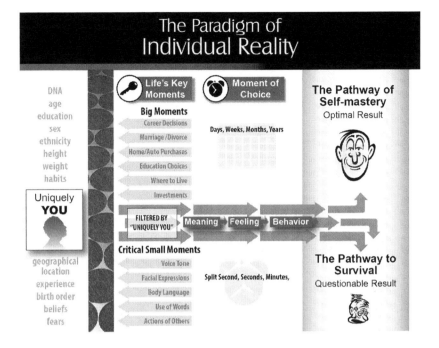

Event ... something that happened, someone said or did something

Meaning ... how you interpreted it through your filter

Feelings ... how it made you feel

Behavior ... what action you decided to take

Result ... how it all turns out for you, it can go many different ways

Something happens or someone says or does something and you apply a meaning, looking through your filter. The meaning you apply creates a feeling, or set of feelings, and as a result, you behave in a certain way, creating a certain result.

The point of this brief conversation is to help you think clearly about who you are, where you are going, and why you are going there. This can give you a template to help you manage your reactions when faced with events, circumstances and people that might cause you to react in a way that may not move you toward the positive results for which you are hoping.

The more you understand who you are and what drives your viewpoints and behavior, the easier it will be for you to understand others.

Step 2.

What's the plan?

Strategy and Corporate Goals

> *There is no "perfect" strategic decision.*
> *The best strategic decision is only an approximation and a risk.*
>
> ~ Peter F. Drucker

It's great to have purpose, values and great mission and vision statements, but you must also have a clear strategy and defined goals.

There are thousands of books, CD's, workshops and webinars about strategy. If you Google strategy you will get 438,000,000 results. There is no shortage of viewpoints about strategy. I will provide an overview of what some of the thinking about strategy is and has been with the objective of giving you an understanding of strategy and some approaches to creating your strategy. I recommend that you do additional reading in this area because the information I provide will not be as detailed as you may find elsewhere. If you do decide to do additional research, you will also find a variety of different approaches with many templates and sophisticated models. My approach will be more simplistic but will be valuable to most of you. See some more viewpoints about strategy in the boxes on the opposite page.

The strategic planning process becomes an end in itself in many corporations. Loads of financial analysts, MBA's, consultants and all kinds of people with strong quantitative skills are called on to do research, projections, build models and develop scenarios about the future. In some of these cases the process becomes very bureaucratic and perhaps irrelevant. The end product of all of this work, which in many cases takes

The Big Lie of Strategic Planning ~Roger L. Martin

The term *strategic planning* is an oxymoron. Planning is about laying out the details of what you intend to do -- how you'll invest existing and new assets and capabilities to reach your targets. But strategy is the step before that -- making difficult and uncomfortable decisions about what targets to aim at in the first place. Too many executives confuse strategy with planning, seeking solace in detailed spreadsheets that project (mythical) costs and revenues far into the future. But if you're entirely comfortable with your strategy, chances are it isn't very good. Rather than the result of careful planning, strategy should arise from a rough-and-ready process. It should start with a simple strategy statement identifying a value proposition that's superior to competitors' – that is, a statement that explains why customers should decide to spend their money with your company and not another. Then, to increase the odds that the strategy will work out, you need to test the logic behind it. Ask yourself, "For this strategy to work, what would have to be true about my customers, the evolution of my industry, my competition, and my own capabilities?" Write down the answers (so you can't rewrite history after the fact). Then if you compare your expectations to what actually happens, you'll be able to see whether your strategy is working or needs to be adjusted. Human nature being what it is, planning will always dominate strategy unless you make a conscious effort to prevent it.

Comments on strategy by Michael Porter, a guru on this subject:

- Competitive strategy is about **being different**. A company outperforms rivals only if it establishes a difference it can preserve.
- **Trade-offs** are essential to strategy. They create the need for choice and purposefully limit what a company offers.
- The essence of strategy is **choosing** what not to do. Strategy renders the choices about what not to do as important as what to do.
- One of the most important functions of strategy is to **guide employees in making choices** that arise in their individual activities and day-to-day decisions.

months and thousands of man-hours, tends to be a series of binders that sit proudly on everyone's bookshelves gathering dust until the annual update, and then they go back on the shelves. In the current environment, these documents are huge electronic files that very few people access. I am perhaps being very unkind in making this statement, but I have personally experienced this behavior and certainly know of many cases where it has not been far off.

> **A Strategy Should Serve as a High-Level Road Map, Which Should Give Structure to the Mission And Vision.**
>
> - It should represent a conscious choice by the organization's leaders to clarify how the organization intends to deliver on its mission over a predefined period of time.
> - It should take into consideration all of the environmental considerations, such as the economy, governmental regulations and others.
> - It should consider the competitive landscape and all the related ramifications.
> - It should be realistic in considering tradeoffs. There is no way to be all things to all people.
> - It should identify the level of risk and be balanced against the corporation's tolerance for risk taking.
> - It should anticipate change and be flexible to changes in any of the impacting factors.
> - It should differentiate the business from known competitors, creating competitive advantage.
> - It must be executable and not a pipe dream.
> - It must engage the entire corporation and allow clear goals to be developed to support its success.

The list in the box is not intended to be exhaustive. It is intended to provide a framework that can be used to help you begin thinking about what a strategy might include, as a starting point.

My viewpoint about strategic planning is that you have to start from where you are. Although that statement sounds very straightforward and easy to understand, not everybody is going to agree with it. If you don't agree with my viewpoint, I suggest that you do whatever additional research you need to do to determine where you believe the start point should be. If you do agree with my viewpoint, then you need to know where you are. You may think you know where you are, but you should clarify your view by immediately doing a SWOT analysis. You should be able to develop a lot of information around the definition of your strengths, weaknesses, opportunities and threats.

If you haven't done a SWOT analysis before you should engage as many people in your organization in the process as reasonably possible. Since your strategy is going to be the next step in building the structure around which you can proceed toward full workforce engagement, getting as much engagement as possible at this point will be productive. Up to this point you have made a good effort to engage as many people as possible and communicate as much as possible, it will be a good idea to continue that process.

I would suggest that the most effective way to get the SWOT analysis done is to do it one piece at a time. As an example, hold a meeting and tell the people at the meeting that you would like to identify as many of your company's strengths as possible. I suggest that you do this simultaneously at as many organizational levels as possible. If you have a small organization, you may want to involve everyone. If you have a larger, more structured organization you may want to engage the management team and get representative input from the other levels in the organization. One of the benefits in taking the project through as many organizational levels as possible is that some people may provide thought-provoking information just because they don't know what they don't know. You will want to provide some examples of what you mean by strengths so everyone is on the same page. Some examples are provided in the box on the next page.

Strengths	*Weaknesses*
• Good image in the market • Produce quality products • Experienced workforce • Responsive to customers • Strong balance sheet • Continually profitable • Etc. etc. etc.	• Inexperienced leadership team • High-cost producer • Limited suppliers • Many workforce members nearing retirement age • High skill level required to produce product • Large percentage of business from a limited number of customers
Opportunities	*Threats*
• Market is still developing • Many competitors are undercapitalized • High-quality products give us a market edge • New leadership team creative and innovative • Available capital to take advantage of market opportunities	• Cost of market entry low • Not a low-cost producer so leaves opportunities for competition • New competitors have newer, more scalable technology • Some risk of product obsolescence

When you have received all of the input, you will need to consolidate the information and come up with a final list. I suggest that you consolidate your final information into a grid or organized list that you can work with. If you have eliminated any input provided, you will want to get back to the people or groups that provided the input and let them know what you have decided to go forward with and why. If you ask people for input and don't use it they deserve to know why. The good or bad news is that you can decide to go forward from this point to develop your strategy, or you can use this base of information to do more research. In either case, before you decide what to do you should ask yourself the following questions:

- **External Environmental Factors.** Do we know enough about the external environmental conditions that could impact us? Considerations might include economic conditions, prices of commodities that can be affected by external factors, governmental regulations, federal, state or local, demographic shifts (baby boomers retiring, millennials coming on strong), availability of labor, potential natural disasters.

- **Competitive Factors.** How much do you know about the competitive landscape? Who are your key competitors and are they getting stronger or weaker? Are products and services being developed that could make your products and services obsolete? Are there new competitors on the horizon? What is the cost of entry in your market; could some new competitor turn up instantly and give you an unwanted surprise? Are any of your competitors able to make internal changes that could make your competitive advantage obsolete?

- **Technology Changes.** What is happening with technology? Are there changes coming that could be extremely beneficial or harmful? How much is happening with technology that you don't understand? How much change can you predict? Where can you get advice to give you more comfort in this area?

- **Internal Considerations.** How do you feel about your organizational structure? Is your culture right? How is your level of communication? How engaged is your workforce? Are you as efficient as you need to be relative to the market demands? Are your systems in place and up to date? Do you have processes in place to respond to unexpected opportunities or threats? Is your leadership team world class? Is your technology current and scalable? Are you a learning organization? Are you keeping key people or is your turnover too high?

We could go on with questions forever. The point of providing this information is to sensitize you to make a conscious decision relative to how much information you need before you develop your strategy.

So Now What Do You Do?

You can proceed any way you think makes sense, but you need to go back and look at your mission and your vision, if you have both. Your strategy needs to be supportive of both your mission and vision. Remember your mission was about what you do now and your vision is about what you want to become.

To be effective your strategy needs to cover more than the current year. You may remember my comments about strategic documents sitting on shelves and gathering dust. Strategic documents that are doing what I described are not live, actionable documents developed by committed people who want to achieve full workforce engagement. My suggestion is that your strategic plan should cover no more than three years with rolling updates. The farther out from today that you project the less likely you are to be accurate. I doubt that you can get comfortable in looking beyond three years and even that may be a stretch.

Remember that you can and should regularly update your strategy for changing conditions that you could not have anticipated, no mater how much research you did. How many people could have predicted the disaster and ramifications of the events of September 11, 2001, three years or three days earlier, or the natural disasters of 2005, or the various things happening around the world at the moment that have far reaching impacts?

In case you are feeling overwhelmed with the prospect of developing a strategy, I would like to share with you how one of my clients developed their strategy. You will find that their process was clean, simple and quick. I won't discuss how much of the process referenced earlier they used, but they did get a strategy in place and communicated it in very short order—just a few days. Here's what they did.

The process was simple. They had already put together their mission/vision. They were a $14 million company and wanted to grow to $50 million in revenue over a five-year period, with a specific margin level. In this case the strategy was put together by the senior leaders and me, with them doing the lion's share of the work.

They started from where they were. They clarified all their revenue sources and looked at the growth of each segment over the recent past, and identified the reason for the rate of growth. This allowed them to project the likely future revenue growth rate from their current customers. They were planning to introduce some new products over the upcoming period, so they decided to differentiate the growth between new products and growth of historic products. They are a very forward-looking and creative-thinking group. They had been working on a few new products, some of which were nearing the reality of market testing.

They decided to project their organic growth forward for five years. They factored in inflation, using the recent historic growth rate, and the likely loss of customers during the period and arrived at a revenue number for the end of the five-year period. This step clarified for them how much additional revenue would need to be generated by new products to arrive at their desired five-year revenue target. Through this logical process, they now were in a position to do the critical thinking and analysis necessary to determine whether the five-year goal was attainable. After a good bit of additional number crunching and what-if scenarios, they reached the conclusion that the goal was attainable. At this point, all they needed to do was flesh out the strategy and the related goals and present it to their team to get the necessary feedback concerning the feasibility of this strategy.

The entire management team agreed that the strategy was doable and the first year goals achievable in the timeframes discussed. The strategy also supported the mission and vision developed earlier. This company's strategy is in place and they developed their current year goals and plan to support the five-year strategy and they are going down the road with high energy. They have created for themselves, and their entire organization, a solid opportunity for success by providing high clarity and strong engagement at all levels.

Now what about you?

You should start by gathering your mission, vision, SWOT analysis grid and the answers to any additional questions you decided to ask yourself after you did the SWOT work. With this information you should be able to start identifying possibilities and working through them. At a minimum, ask yourself the questions in the box on the next page.

Mission, Vision and Strategy Questions

- Are there financial targets we would like to achieve in the planning timeframe, such as revenue, profit margin and others?
- Which of our strengths can we capitalize on to drive competitive advantage in the marketplace?
- What opportunities can we take advantage of and maximize?
- What steps can we take to shore up any areas of weakness that could inhibit us from reaching our goals?
- What steps can we take to avoid or eliminate any threats we see?
- How much risk are we willing to take?

Each of the above questions should lead to other questions. Your task will be to answer the above and other questions sufficiently to allow you to clearly and crisply identify what your strategy will be. You may find the process as clear and simple as the client I described above, or it may be much more complex for you. Remember that you don't have a crystal ball and you can't predict the future with 100-percent accuracy. You are trying to look ahead, with as much clarity as possible, and take advantage of where you are to maximize your success. Also keep in mind that things will change and you will not always get it right the first time. The strategy you are developing is a living document not a dust collector. It is being designed by you to provide a plan with the best thinking possible for moving forward to deliver on your mission and toward the realization of your vision.

If you have followed the process outlined above and engaged everyone in the development of the strategy, you will have a living document.

We have not talked specifically about goals in this section. We will talk in more detail about goals and how to set them and how they can impact the engagement of the workforce in Step 3. However, company high-level goals need to be established for at least the first year of the strategic plan. Without clear company goals it will be impossible to focus, allocate resources and engage and align the organization.

It may be relatively easy to establish clear financial goals for the period if you have done a good job with the strategic plan. The financial goals may also get a lion's share of your focus throughout the year as you do monthly and quarterly reviews and make adjustments as necessary.

Development of your financial goals may start with a review of the prior year or the trend over the past few years, but will be driven primarily by your upcoming year revenue forecast. The revenue forecast will allow you to develop the cost side of your upcoming year financial plan (budget), which will support achieving your profit goals. We are not going to talk about capital plans or even detailed budgeting, but you will no doubt want to generate a revenue goal and a profit goal. To do this you will need to at least complete a good revenue and cost forecast as described briefly on the opposite page.

In addition to your financial goals, you may want to develop goals in a variety of additional areas including the following:

- **Process and procedure enhancements**—what new or improved tools and systems do you need?
- **People development goals**—how will you support the learning and growth of your team?
- **Client retention and satisfaction**—what will you need to do to keep your clients on board and happy?

Financial, clients, people and processes are the four key areas of the balanced scorecard concept. It is up to you how many goals you have and in what areas, but the four performance areas outlined above are all core to your continued business success. You may also want to apply the idea that less is more to your goal setting and keep the number of goals as small as possible. A good target might be five goals or less that you can really focus on and measure performance against clearly.

Now more bits and pieces for you

What's your strategy? Do you have a life plan, at least at a high level? Where do you want to be personally in 5, 10, 15 years? Is there an overall plan? Has there ever been one, or have you arrived where you are by accident? I doubt that you are where you are totally by accident, but I would guess that life has had some unexpected twists and turns. Do you believe that you should sit back and wait to be handed a deck of cards and then decide how to play them? Is there something you can do about your life direction? I don't intend to answer this question, but it gets posed often, and there are many different viewpoints about what, if anything, you should do about it.

If you determine your purpose, values, mission and vision, do you then need a strategy and some clear goals? It's a good question that only you can answer.

STEP 3.

What do you want from me and where do I fit?

Goal Setting and Alignment

We have arrived at the point where we get specific about where we are going, and how to get there. In the earlier steps we discussed where we are headed in the short term, and where we want to go in the longer term. We are now going to start talking about the details of the journey and what part everyone plays.

How many times do you leave the house in your car without a destination in mind? If you are going to a new location do you leave without a map or some kind of directions? Do you at least know that you can get specific help from your smartphone or you car's GPS?

I have heard it said that Americans are obsessive about measuring everything. I don't know if that is true, but I suspect that most of you reading this book measure many things in your life whether you have thought about it or not. Think about grades when you were in school or about the various competitive sports you participate in or have participated in. How about your weight and fitness level? Does anyone who is reading this book find that they judge their own standard of success by the amount and kind of things they have, relative to others. Don't we have a strong desire to always know how we are doing compared to some standard? I am convinced we do. How does a company administer a pay-for-performance program if they don't know what performance is or how to measure it? How can workers earn extra pay for extra performance if they don't know what extra means and how to measure it?

Flip back and look at the title of this chapter again. How can you expect to engage your workforce if they don't know what you want from them and where they fit?

This segment of our journey is all about goals. The chapter title is "What do you want from me and where do I fit?" That may sound like two distinct things but they are tightly interrelated. You will see how that is the case as we go forward.

Although I have a graduate degree in business, I managed to graduate without having any exposure to goal setting, how to do it, how important it is, or anything at all.

I started my career in sales and had lots of training around product knowledge, sales techniques and related areas. I also had some sales goals, or at least a specific number of calls to make. I was young, excited, inexperienced and wanting to do well. So I went out and worked as hard and fast as I could in my territory to do whatever I was told or seemed important. I did well enough to be promoted to a senior sales rep quickly, with no more clarity about what that meant, but I continued to work hard and got a little raise so things were going well. I decided pretty early on that I wanted to manage people; why I don't know, but I did. It became clear to me that getting into a management position in sales was going to be a long wait because of the low rate of turnover and the number of people standing in line ahead of me. Being a sales manager was a good job in this company at the time.

Since I was happy there, I started poking around to see where there might be opportunities for me to manage people in other parts of the company. The company had an internal job posting process so I was able to stay on top of what other kinds of jobs were around. As luck would have it, I was able to find a supervisory position in another part of the company in another city and tossed my hat in the ring. I eventually got the job, moved, and had my first supervisory position since finishing graduate school. The good news is that I had a good deal of experience supervising people from a variety of jobs I held while in college. The other news is that if I hadn't had the earlier supervisory experience, I might have been in deep trouble because I received zero training for my first position as a supervisor in a corporate accounting function. Yes I had accounting and finance classes in undergraduate and graduate school, but it wasn't what I had planned on doing and the classes didn't give me any tools to help me understand how to manage or lead a group of people.

Are you wondering what this story about my career has to do with goals? It only serves to get me to a place where I can tell you how I got engaged in my lifelong involvement in understanding the importance of goals.

I was fortunate enough to be promoted a couple of times in corporate accounting and found myself as a 25-year-old manager of an accounting function with five supervisors, 70 employees, two departments and responsibility for processing thousands of transactions, representing millions of dollars in an area that I knew little about.

At a point about midway through my trip through corporate accounting, the company introduced a new management by objectives program. There you go, now we are back to goals. I had not been exposed to management by objectives while in college so this was a new and exciting thing for me. I immediately went out and bought some books on the subject and gained a little knowledge so I could make the best of this new MBO process.

My learning experience from the company was interesting. They did a very good job of providing all of the materials and appropriate training for how the program was supposed to work. This was a company-wide program from the corporate office in New York so it got all the appropriate attention. We implemented the program and off we went. I was excited about all this and became a bit of a zealot. I engaged all of my management team members and we were going for it with high energy.

After a few months of using the system, the communication and high energy around the project from the corporate office seemed to disappear throughout the company. I also noticed that my boss lost interest in using the system and the whole thing died a quiet death throughout the company, except not with me. I found that the whole MBO concept made sense. However, I also found that the system given to me was very cumbersome to use. There was too much emphasis on balancing and cross-footing numbers and filling in boxes, and not enough emphasis on some things that I had found to be more important, like performance-related communication and discussions about career possibilities and other things.

I decided to continue to use the system, but with some major modifications. This introduction to the MBO concept (not specifically MBO, but the concept), is what started me down the road to a lifetime of commitment to, and continual refinement of, how to use goals in maximizing human performance. At the time of writing this book, I have used and been training other people to use some version of this system for over 35 years. I've had consistent success without regard to organizational level or who my boss was or who my clients are.

But before I introduce you to my system of goal setting, tracking and feedback, I want to do two other things. I would be remiss if I didn't make some additional comments about the most widely used system called "the balanced scorecard." This system was developed by Robert Kaplan and David Norton and is well documented in their book by the same name, first published in 1996. I encourage anyone who is reading this book to also read "The Balanced Scorecard" and the current updates and understand the balanced scorecard concept.

The second thing I will do is discuss the topic of goals. Once again I want to emphasize the importance of goals. Why start the trip if we don't have a destination in mind? How do you expect your team members to perform if they don't know what is expected of them or how to measure their success? If you are a big fan of pay-for-performance for some positions, as many people are today, how will you make that work without goal clarity?

Effective Goals Have Five Key Characteristics (SMART)

1. They are Specific and clear with enough detail to be easily understood and agreed to by the person accountable for achieving them.

2. They are Measurable in a manner that is easily understood, such as due dates, performance metrics, financial measures and quality measures.

3. They are Achievable with a stretch. No walk in the park but also not so much blue sky that there is no hope.

4. They are Results-oriented, meaning that they need to tie in to and support the overall goals of the company, department, division or other organizational level.

5. They must be Time-sensitive. It will be important that they be completed within time-based guidelines.

There has been much written about goals, and most of it is much more complex than what I have just identified. I encourage you to read all the other definitions and approaches and I challenge you to find anything that adds value beyond these five simple requirements: specific, measurable, achievable, results-oriented and time-sensitive. Most discussions will come down to these five things, and they may also be part of a larger system like the balanced scorecard system.

For goals to be valuable they must be part of a larger system or process. Goals, just for the sake of goals, may well add value, but the value may be small compared to the value they can add if they are part of a more robust system. It won't make much sense for people to have goals if achieving them doesn't get the overall business to its goals. When I refer to goals being part of a larger system, I am talking about the way goals are set, who is involved and how the goals of the organization tie together at all levels to create a line of sight for every team member.

Part of this chapter, as the title says, is about, "where do I fit," or what is the line of sight from my goals to the goals of the entire organization? An important part of setting goals is determining how any specific individual's or department's goals fit in with the overall goals of the enterprise, or at least, the next level of the organization to which they are responsible. The alignment of goals from top to bottom is critical to optimize engagement and bottom-line results.

The best result will be achieved when everybody at every level of the organization understands how what they do contributes to the overall success of the enterprise. An effective goal-setting process has three clear steps.

The boss, whether she/he is the owner, CEO, division head, department director, manager or supervisor of a function must follow three steps:

The Process

1. Leader defines goals. Clearly define a series of four to six goals that his/her organization will focus on over the next measurement period, which is usually a calendar or fiscal year. If you are not the owner or CEO you should make every effort to assure that the goals you are setting tie into and support the goals of the company. With these goals, you must also define the measurement system so you will be able to determine when you have been successful. It is important that the measurement

system be accessible and understandable with no ambiguity. The success of your performance management process will be greatly diminished if there are arguments about what successful performance looks like.

2. Leader meets with the next level to discuss the goals and the process. Set up a meeting with your subordinate team to discuss your goals and how they will be measured and why they are important. Provide a copy of your goals to your team far enough ahead of the meeting to allow the team time to think about how to design their goals to tie into and work well with yours. This will be a good opportunity for you to be sure that everyone clearly understands the goal-setting process, your goals and how your goals, if you are not the CEO or owner, fit with the company goals. The objective of this meeting is for everyone to leave the meeting understanding your goals and how they should go about setting their own goals. It must also be clear that it will be their responsibility to set their own goals to tie in with yours. Although their goals will obviously be more specific than yours and have different elements, they must ultimately tie in to yours.

3. Leader and subordinates finalize goals and sign off indicating mutual support. Have a final meeting with your subordinates, individually, to finalize each of their goals. Be sure that you and each of your subordinates clearly understand the goals, the measurement system, and that all of the goals meet the five key points for effective goal setting. You may want to consider spending some additional time at this point to be sure that each of your team feels that the goals have come from them and that they are achievable, with a stretch. It is also important that they are willing to be held accountable for achieving them. To indicate mutual commitment to the goals, you and each of your subordinates should sign the goal statement indicating that you are in it together. This will help clarify that the goals are not being developed as a method to micromanage or punish. They are designed to focus the organization in one direction and allow for clear communication, alignment and mutual commitment.

Underlying any performance management system is the concept of accountability and consequences. There is little value in having an organized system of goal setting from top to bottom with alignment and a clear line of sight, if you don't have a culture of accountability and consequences. We will talk more about recognition and rewards in Step 5, but it is worth discussing here the importance of consequences. Although I believe that everyone wants to do the best they can, it is my view that there will occasionally be people who are in the actively disengaged group we discussed in the overview. Even though the underlying reason we are discussing the **seven steps** is to help you achieve maximum engagement of your workforce, it is likely that getting to 100-percent full engagement will be challenging. If you do not have clarity about what is expected, who is accountable for what and the consequences for non-performance, you will have a much larger challenge than you want in trying to deal with those team members who are not making the necessary effort to achieve their goals.

I have worked with clients who do everything possible to keep their employees informed and always show the positive side and wonder why they are not getting the results they want. In some cases this may be happening due to lack of clear goals or some gap in the goal-setting system. There are, however, more than enough examples of companies allowing cultures of no consequences to exist. Although it is very difficult, particularly in a small family oriented culture, to apply consequences to poor performance, it is required for the ultimate success of the company.

Allowing a member, or members, of the team to continually get away with obvious non-performance sets a very bad example for the rest of the team and will eventually cause low morale, turnover and lost customers. In this kind of environment the low performers will stay and the high performers will go to the competition and the environment will become progressively worse with the percent of fully engaged employees going down and the not engaged and actively disengaged becoming the norm.

It is very important to get the goal-setting process right in your company. My experience is that even if you agree with what I am saying and you decide to put this process in place, it will take more focus than you may envision. However, once you have a solid performance management system in place for a year or two, it will function very smoothly and consume much less time, assuming you keep it fresh.

The area where the process has a tendency to fall apart is as you rely on your subordinate team to cascade the goals throughout the rest of your organization. This can become a particularly interesting challenge if you are involved in a large organization. There is only one way to avoid this tendency.

You must stay active in the goal-setting, follow-up and feedback process until it is ingrained in your organization. There is no other way. The good news, it's not as hard as it may seem. All you need to do as you walk around being visible in your organization is ask to see a set of the goals for everyone on the team as you visit them. It's a rational request and makes it clear that you are serious about goal setting and performance against those goals

You will have to do this a few times early in the life of the process. Once you have gone through a full year cycle or two of this process your team will have seen your commitment and their results and they will own the process.

Action Planning

You must develop great SMART goals but it is entirely another thing to achieve them even if you are highly engaged. Goals will be very difficult to achieve without specific action plans. I have experienced management team members assuring me that they didn't need to develop and record action plans since they are competent, capable adults. In cases when I have acquiesced I have found they have been incorrect, as the urgency of the day's work overcomes the actions that need to be taken to achieve goals and they are often missed. Although action planning seems like a no brainer, if it doesn't get the proper emphasis and focus it won't get done and goals will not be achieved. I have found that even in today's environment of technology solutions for most things, many people still find it useful to develop and print out action plans and keep them visible to help them stay on track. Don't undervalue action plans.

As I have traveled through my career as a business leader, corporate executive, executive coach and consultant, I have found that the implementation of this process is the single most important tool for success, without regard for organization size, structure, product or service. I have also found that once the people who have worked with or for me actually put this process in place, they are never satisfied to manage without it as they go forward in their careers or businesses.

Now more bits and pieces for you

If you decide to create a personal strategy then perhaps you need to have some goals to support that strategy. Can you really get through life with no goals? If you have managed to get to the age you are now and have had no goals, I would like to know how you have done it. If you have had goals before, I assume you may have some now. If you plan to have goals to support your strategy, I would encourage you to think about your goals with the questions in the box in mind.

Personal Goal Thinking

- What are you really trying to achieve?
- How will the achievement of these goals serve you?
- When you look back from 5 or 10 years out, will you be happy with your goal selection today?
- Who else do you need to consider in setting these goals?
- Will you be proud of these goals?
- Is this all there is?

Think about it.

STEP 4.

How do I know how I am doing?

Performance Feedback

What are the areas of our lives in which we do not keep some kind of score? Hopefully, there are some, otherwise we may be a bit out of balance. However, the areas where we do keep score are countless. In many of these areas we don't need instant feedback and in others we do. Feedback allows us to adjust our behavior and perhaps our performance in time to make a difference. We may not get to do over what we just did, but we do have more information about how we might get a better result the next time with different efforts or inputs. I believe you would agree, there are many things about our lives and experiences that would not be nearly as interesting if we didn't have a way to keep score and get feedback on the results.

Isn't our business, our job or our career a big part of our lives? The obvious answer is yes. I wonder then if it isn't very important to receive feedback about how we are doing. We have already discussed the importance of goals and why having goals with the right kind of feedback at the right frequency is important.

The best way to get performance feedback is through the job itself. There are many jobs where regular feedback from the job itself is possible. In many cases the feedback is available to the person doing the job but perhaps not to the boss. Sometimes this feedback will come from a customer, either live or on the phone, or perhaps in a production environment from the machine, or in a sales environment from making the sale, or in a project environment from the completion of the project on time and within standards. We all grow up with measurement and feedback.

Doesn't our education system provide us with instant feedback? Students are tested on a very regular basis, isn't that just a measurement and feedback system? If they didn't get test scores and eventually grades would their effort and learning be the same? I guess there is a lot of debate about this in educational circles, but for now I suspect there will continue to be tests and grades to provide feedback about levels of learning and opportunities for improvement. In today's environment with the competition for spots at institutions of higher education it seems that grades (measurement and feedback) are more important than ever.

If you are running a business or a department it will be in your best interest to find methods for your team to get solid, accurate and regular performance feedback on as frequent a basis as possible.

There are plenty of theories about how frequently employees should receive some form of formal, written performance reviews. Many companies do a formal review once per year. There are others that do none, and there are plenty who have a formal program to do reviews once per year but they don't actually happen. There are others that have a system for doing semi-annual or quarterly reviews and in many cases they just don't happen. What happens in your company and how do you know?

It has been rare in my experience to see companies doing a great job of doing formal performance reviews on any frequency other than annual. In many cases even those are cursory and done to allow for the paperwork to be in a file to justify, or not justify, a compensation adjustment.

I believe there are many ways people get feedback, including their boss telling them what kind of a job they are doing. Feedback can be very frequent or rare and the environment can be formal or informal, from written input to quick words while passing in the hallway. Although any and all feedback is valuable, formal feedback documented in writing is always taken more seriously than any other kind. To maximize performance, feedback needs to be taken seriously and have meaning.

Formal performance reviews of some kind should be done at least quarterly. I might be inclined to suggest that it should be monthly, but I know that monthly may be too big a challenge. Some small business leaders who are reading this may be thinking, "you must be kidding me, monthly, no hope; quarterly, fat chance; annually, yea I hope to get to it." Hopefully, those kinds of thoughts or actions wouldn't come from the majority and I'm hoping you are converted after reading this book.

Those of you that are leaders at larger companies are probably doing whatever your company requires you to do. In your case, I suggest that, unless your company is having you do a formal quarterly review, you take it up a notch and do it on your own with your team at least quarterly.

Think about this issue. How can you possibly think that doing a formal review once per year is adequate? Yes, I know you have all kinds of performance-related discussions throughout the year on an informal basis. How do you remember all of those conversations at the end of the year? Is there a chance that if you only do a formal appraisal once per year that you are inclined to be measuring what happened the last quarter? You may vaguely remember some performance issues from earlier in the year but they may be a fading memory. Perhaps none of this matters if your annual review is nothing other than a formality. Perhaps your annual review process is one of those that checks boxes or rates characteristics on a scale of 1 to 5. Does rating characteristics do anything for anybody? Is there something to be learned or changed and does anybody really care? Is this process really providing positive feedback about performance against clear goals that can lead to positive change? Do you use some kind of a ranking system that creates competition versus teamwork? What impact is that having on your workforce?

If you have put in place a solid set of goals, as discussed earlier, and the related action plans, I suggest that you now have the framework to support positive performance. You will also be providing the members of your team the opportunity to get great satisfaction from seeing the results of their performance. The best way to make your goal setting system come alive and work for you and your team is through a process of formal reviews at least quarterly.

As the leader of your company, division or department your demonstration of your commitment to providing formal performance feedback, on at least a quarterly basis, will make the process successful or not. The following steps will make the difference:

The Process Continued

1. Define the requirement. Declare that quarterly formal performance reviews will be the standard operating procedure for your company, department or division. And that you will be doing reviews throughout the organization. You will obviously want to provide the logic behind your decision and get the buy-in of the team. Whether you get immediate and full buy-in or

not, it will be worth your effort to go forward.

2. Introduce the process. Introduce the record-keeping system. You may want to create an electronic record-keeping system that is comfortable for you. I suggest that, at a minimum, you follow the easy-to-use, manual system that I used for over 35 years. Provide each of your direct reports with a three-ring binder with their names on the spine and your company or department name on the cover. If your performance management system has a name or theme include it. The binders should have enough dividers for each of your direct reports' subordinates. In the front of each section will be the goals of your direct reports and in the following sections will be the goals of her/his direct reports. You will, of course, have the same kind of binder for yourself. Explain that the purpose of the binder is to track, record and discuss performance results each quarter and how the process will work. Yes. I know this sounds antiquated and it is. My point is the logic is the same between systems and I encourage you to use whatever system is best for your environment. In fact, designing a system that works for you or finding an off-the-shelf electronic system that everyone can easily use will support the effective use of the system.

3. Put the system to work. You will meet with each of your subordinates individually on a quarterly basis and take the following actions:

    - Each quarter determine and record performance results to date against agreed goals. Some of the goals may not be due each quarter, but this review will give you a good opportunity to understand where projects stand. If the subordinate has performance measures based on regular metrics, such as profit and loss results or service standards, for example, there will be plenty of results to discuss. Each review may involve a combination of goals based on project completions and those based on regular performance metrics.

    - Congratulate your subordinate for the successes he/she has experienced during the most recent quarter. If there are goal areas that are not on target, record these and have a discussion about them. Your discussion should center around the reasons for the missed goals, what is being done to get back on track, and when it is anticipated that performance will be back on track. All issues that have impacted performance should be recorded. If there are issues that are acceptable reasons for subpar performance, those should be discussed and recorded as well. You should also discuss whether the subordinate needs something from you that they are not getting. Perhaps they need additional tools or more personal involvement or support from you.

- Identify and record special projects, or special efforts, that have been expended during the measurement period that are clearly above and beyond the agreed on goals. This is another good opportunity for you to recognize good performance.

- Use these reviews to surface issues that either you or the team member you are reviewing has. This is a good time to discuss real issues like career progress, road blocks of which you are not aware, resource challenges, leadership styles and development opportunities. The environment created by the quarterly formal review is conducive to open and productive discussions.

It is important that the necessary time be spent to discuss performance for the period in good detail and that everything appropriate is recorded. Both you, and each of your subordinates, should leave each of these quarterly meetings with complete clarity about where they stand and anything they need to do and need from you to get back on track, if they are not on target.

By using this tracking and feedback system, you will assure that at the end of the period—whatever the period is—you will have a clear, written record of performance. This will allow you to complete an annual review, if you have one, objectively and fairly, rather than be influenced by the most recent quarter's performance or what you can remember from earlier in the year. It will also provide the opportunity for complete clarity and course correction, if necessary, throughout the year while making adjustments can still make a difference.

Once again, I cannot emphasize enough the importance of establishing clear goals, action plans and performance tracking using the method discussed or a method that fits better for your culture. Establishing clarity about performance results and providing feedback on a regular basis is a very key issue to achieving workforce engagement.

Now more bits and pieces for you

How will you measure your personal success? Is your success measured in financial terms? Do you believe that the person who dies with the most toys wins? It is important for you to get some clarity around how you are going to measure success. The measurements should be tied to the goals discussed earlier but they may change as time goes on and circumstances change. How will you know if you are being a good wife, husband, father, leader, employee or friend? Dose it matter? Perhaps it does, only you can decide.

It may be important that you just pay attention to what you use as your measuring stick or sticks. It's very easy and somewhat normal to use tangible things such as money, cars, homes and all the other things I don't need to mention. What about your health? How will you know how you are doing? Did your health make it into your goals? If you don't have your health, what do you have? Would you measure your health by the length of time between doctor visits, how far you can run, how many sit-ups you can do? Who knows, but it may be valuable to find a way to measure it and put a value on it.

At the end of the day, the best way to measure how you are doing is to look in the mirror. If you honestly like what you see you are probably on the right track.

STEP 5.

What's in it for me ... WIFM?

Recognition, Rewards, Appreciation and Feeling Successful

No matter how you slice it, everyone needs to make a living. There have been constant studies about the importance of compensation, recognition and rewards, for as long as I can remember. These studies and research projects continue today and it seems like there is a new one every week. I have not been able to find one system that has all the answers, the silver bullet of compensation, recognition and rewards. Many years ago I attended a presentation by Fredrick W. Herzberg. After attending the presentation I did some additional research and found his philosophy extremely interesting.

Fred believed that in motivating people there are satisfiers and dissatisfiers. The dissatisfiers are things like the immediate work area, the employee eating facility, the location of parking, cleanliness of the facility, access to tools, policies and procedures, the direct supervisor and base compensation. Satisfiers are things like achievement, recognition, advancement, responsibility and the job itself, to name a few. It was Fred's belief that until you eliminate, or show evidence that you have recognized and are working on solving the dissatisfiers, you will not make much progress on the satisfiers, which are the real motivators.

An Experiment in Motivation

After attending the presentation by Fred Herzberg, and doing a bit more research about his philosophies, I had the opportunity to test some of his beliefs. I was a supervisor in a large accounting department at the time. There were about eight other men and women in the same front-level supervisory role at the time. All of us were supervising 10 to 15 people, primarily female, doing basic accounting processes associated with billing and collection. All of the supervisors were young and were always looking for methods to get more productivity from our teams. We had reasonably good methods for tracking performance, so we could tell when we made any progress in productivity.

I convinced my peers to join me in my experiment using Fred's philosophy. Let me describe the work environment so you can envision the circumstances. There were 100-plus people all working in one large room on the fourth floor of an old building. There was a director's office in one corner, two managers' offices and the rest of the area contained rows of desks with a supervisor for every 10 to 15 people. Visualize the rows of desks. The desks were the old military style, with rubber-type-tops and gray sides, and each one had a gray wastebasket. The floors were a beige tile and the walls were an off-white. There were occasional windows, no art on the wall, and file cabinets all over the place, many times in front of the limited windows. By the way, this was not a new building, Sounds great doesn't it?

My peers and I agreed to come in one weekend, while the office was closed.

We came in and washed all the desks and walls, cleaned the floor, made what adjustments we could to the light in the room, moved a few file cabinets away from windows where we could to allow for more light, and washed and painted the wastebaskets light beige. We also found some brightly colored travel posters (we were in the travel industry), had them framed and mounted them on the wall, and capped our efforts off with a bud vase and flower on every desk.

On the Monday morning following the weekend we were all waiting wondering what would happen. The people came in and were overwhelmed. Productivity for the day was trashed. There was so much conversation about the change that there wasn't much real work done, but there was an incredible amount of positive conversation about the changes. As we moved forward we experienced a measurable, immediate productivity gain that averaged 30-40 percent over the next 120 days, and leveled off and stayed at about 25 percent over time. In addition to the gains in productivity, the positive communication between management and the workforce increased dramatically, resulting in many positive suggestions that helped reduce costs while also achieving the productivity gains.

The results from this experiment were very impressive to me and the rest of the team. As you might guess, as a young management team, we all went on with our careers in different directions in the company, or on to other companies and different locations in the world. I am unable to vouch for the long-term impact of the Herzberg experience on any of my peers. For me it was life changing. It was the start of my journey down a road of continual interest and study relative to human behavior in the workplace and the impact on productivity,

Back to the reason for this brief digression. The reason for the positive results we experienced was nothing more than recognition. We had recognized the drab and boring workplace and how the workforce might feel and did something about it. We had taken the time to think about the people who worked with us and made the effort to make their work environment more enjoyable. We had recognized them as people, not cogs in a corporate wheel. The results we experienced were outstanding and the cost no more than a weekend of personal time, a few dollars for cleaning materials, paint and a few poster frames. Fundamentally we had answered one small WIFM (what's in it for me) question. We had demonstrated that we cared.

When trying to address the WIFM question, there are some fundamentals that have to be in place. You must have a salary and benefits combination that is viewed as fair by the people working for you. It must be seen as fair compared to available compensation plans in the industry and location, and it must be viewed as fair between the individuals within your company. The thing I didn't mention when discussing the Herzberg research is that salary will usually not be a satisfier, but can be a dissatisfier. There is plenty of research available showing that salary is rarely the key driver of workforce performance or retention. You must, however, be at parity with your competition if you hope to attract and retain a talented workforce.

A Few Words about Base Compensation

The key with salary programs is to assure that they are considered fair. I'm not prepared to discuss here how you should establish salaries other than that they must be considered fair by all levels in the workforce. There is a great deal of research on compensation, including frequent salary studies by job classification and location. Organizations like the Society for Human Resource Management, state and federal agencies and many private companies, and trade associations do extensive research in this area. There are a variety of good online tools as well. This is a topic you must stay on top of. In most companies the topic of how much and how people are paid is kept confidential. The reality is that salaries get out. It is always a mystery but they do. You may as well accept this reality and assure that your process is fair.

I have found over the years that one way to create some feeling of fairness is to establish and publish salary ranges. There are no doubt reasons why you may or may not want to do this, but if you do, I believe there are more up sides than down sides. If you decide to publish ranges it will require that you think clearly about what each job is worth. To do this you will need to do the necessary research to assure that you are competitive. If ranges are published and considered fair by your employee group, you will find that there will be less conversation about specific salaries since everyone will know, or at least have access to, the information about how they broadly stack up with peers, subordinates and bosses. I don't believe there are any significant downsides to publishing ranges if your company is one that operates from a base of integrity and openness.

What about Benefits?

The question then comes up about benefits. I believe the conceptual framework related to benefits is similar to that of salary determination. You can't be out of whack with the rest of your industry and expect to attract and retain solid talent. There are plenty of regulations today that make it challenging to discriminate in your benefit offerings. Yes, there are some things you can do that are different between exempt and non-exempt and management and non-management, but there are plenty of constraints. The key is to determine the amount of dollars you can afford to spend on benefits and then craft the most favorable combination of benefits for your workforce. I suggest that before deciding on what benefits to offer, you do the necessary research to understand what is possible. There is a good deal of information available both online and through consultants and industry associations. I suggest that you take advantage of all the research that is available. Don't forget that many organizations that provide benefit programs have a great deal of research available as well.

Depending on how you feel about engaging your workforce in this process, you may want to gather as much information as possible from them on this topic. I suggest that the risk of doing this is to raise their expectations, so you may want to do as much research as possible and understand your spending limits prior to engaging them. Although I have raised this caution, I am a very big fan of getting as much input as possible from the people who will be impacted by your decisions.

It will be important to get your base salary and benefit programs sorted out before going any further. Once you get these two issues well in hand, you may want to consider whether or not you want to have any kind of gain-sharing process. When I use the words, gain-sharing, I am talking about performance-based incentives such as bonuses, profit sharing, stock or stock options, and the many variations of pay-for-performance options.

There is no doubt that if you can create the correct line of sight from every job in your company to the impact on the bottom line, and then reward exceptional performance, you will be ahead of the game if you are doing this for the right positions.

Providing the correct pay-for-performance plan will clearly go a long way toward answering the WIFM question. The trick is to be able to do it and do it well. In my view, one of the better approaches to achieving this is the practice of open-book management. If you are not familiar with the concept, I suggest that you read the books that have been written by Jack Stack, who started the open-book management movement. Jack's first book is called "The Great Game of Business" and the second is called "A Stake in the Outcome." There have been a variety of books published by other authors in between these two and many since that are worth reading. If you are willing to totally share your company financial information with ALL of your employees, take the time to educate them on how to understand it, and give them a financial stake in what they produce, you will see excellent results.

Jack's story is a good one and has been the source for the founding of a variety of companies and the personal success of a great number of individuals. Sharing 100 percent of your financial information, training everyone in your company on how the income statement, balance sheet and cash flow statement work, letting them know how what they do impacts the result, and then giving them a stake in the outcome, is the most extreme example of the use of incentive compensation. It is also likely the most effective. You may or may not be ready for this approach, but it is clearly worth your time to research the concept and understand why you do or don't want to do it. Creating this kind of an opportunity for your workforce is more about emotional engagement than about immediate monetary gain.

Pay for Performance

There are a wide variety of options when it comes to offering pay-for-performance systems. There is everything from doing nothing to going to a full-blown, open-book management process. You can share what your employees produce in a variety of ways, from issuing stock and/or stock options to providing profit sharing to bonus programs. The key to the success of whatever incentive program you decide to put in place will be driven by answering these questions.

> **Answering the questions below and responding correctly will help you achieve success with any incentive programs you develop.**
>
> 1. Is the program fair to all concerned, in every way?
> 2. Is the program easy to understand and communicate?
> 3. Is the program easy to maintain, as you move forward?
> 4. Will the program clearly achieve your financial goals when the individual performance goals are met?
> 5. Is the program easy to administer?
> 6. Are the payouts frequent enough to allow the employee to connect the performance results to the payout?
> 7. Are you willing to have the program run for a good long time?
> 8. Is the program self funding, will the results cover the cost?
> 9. Is the program supportive of the current understanding of the positive and negative effects of incentive-based compensation?

The questions on the table assume that you have created the correct line of sight between the performance and the result, and that you plan to have a major communication effort to introduce the program.

You may find that to effectively answer all of the above questions you will want to start with a simple program that generates a bonus of some kind based on clear improvements in sales or reduction of expenses. You can usually put this kind of a program together on your own and achieve success with it. Whatever you decide to do you will want to start with something very simple and something you are fairly sure will pay out results quickly. If your workforce is unable to achieve results quickly, they may well lose interest and all of your work and good intent may be wasted.

Please take the time to do as much research as possible to give yourself a good base of information to start from before you put any program in place.

Do incentives really work? Recent research by Dan Pink raises the question relative to whether or not incentives really work and, if so, for what kinds of positions. Research presented by Dan in his book "Drive" and his TED Talks, makes the case that incentives can drive worse performance, not better performance. He makes a case that in today's complex work environment where the most valued commodity is intellectual capability, incentives may backfire. He makes the case that it is intrinsic motivation (inside out) as opposed to external motivation (outside in) that drives performance. I suggest that before implementing an incentive program of any kind you read "Drive" and consider Dan Pink's presentation of current research results.

Since salary, financial incentives and benefits will not fully answer the WIFM question, we will spend a bit of time discussing other forms of rewards and recognition.

There are probably as many ways to recognize, reward and show appreciation for people as there are people. Before we talk about rewards and recognition, I have another bit of information for you. The U.S. Department of Labor recently reported that the number one reason people leave their jobs is because "they don't feel appreciated." If retention is an issue for you, the next few paragraphs may be highly valuable.

Recognition Is Often FREE

Let's start with the simplest form of recognition, the thank you. A recent survey by the Gallup Organization found that 61 percent of employees claim they haven't received a meaningful "Atta boy!" in the past year. Perhaps you are wondering how that could be possible. When is the last time you had one compared to the last time you did a good job, or perhaps even great job? When is the last time you gave one?

It's easy to get on with the business of business and forget that sometimes it's the little things that count the most. How much closer could you get to the full engagement of your workforce if you took the time to say thank you more often? Don't finish reading this and go out there and start thanking everyone because they will feel your insincerity. If reading this has caused you to think about the value of thanking people for doing a good job and you think you have been underperforming, give it some thought and decide how you want to approach making a change.

If you want to do a better job of thanking people for doing a good job think about how you are going to do it. One of the key issues in making a thank you feel valuable to an employee is to assure that it is specific to something they did recently and communicating why it was a valuable contribution. The more specific the better, and the closer to the performance even better. As an example, which of the following comments do you think will have the most positive impact? "Bob, thanks for doing a good job last week" or "Bob, the research report you put together last week was critical to our success in getting the XYZ account. Great job. Thanks very much."

Either one of these thank you methods might be more than Bob is used to getting, but one is certainly more personal than the other and demonstrates your engagement with the business and recognition of Bob's specific contribution.

I don't want to spend a great deal of time talking about this topic.

I do, however, want to assure you that the value of the personal and specific thank you for doing a great job will have a higher return on your investment than any other form of recognition you can dream up or find and use.

Your cost for this investment is essentially zero. Perhaps a little research about the performance of your own employees will pay big dividends. I also believe that you will find that the return in terms of how making this effort makes you feel will make you have a better day.

What Recognition Programs Work?

You may be wondering what kind of recognition programs work. That's actually a very good question and, once again, there has been a good deal of research on this topic. Rather than spending time on recognition and reward programs, I would rather talk about how they might be used and implemented. The first thing to think about in any recognition or reward program is what are you trying to achieve by implementing the program? Is there an associated business objective? Are you trying to increase revenue, reduce costs, improve attendance, improve your safety record, reduce turnover, improve retention, stimulate new employee referrals, improve project turnaround times, improve time to market with a new product, reduce inventory costs or improve the receivables? The list of things you may want to tie to a recognition or reward program could be endless. The point is you need to tie these programs to some business objective so you can recognize the achievement and how it supports business goals. Even the longstanding recognition for long service is designed to recognize loyalty and aid retention.

What do you think about the employee of the month programs that are prevalent in companies of all sizes? There are plenty of them around in large and small companies. Does that mean they are good and produce value? Are they tied to the companies' business goals? I can't answer these questions and suspect that you can't either, unless you have one going in your company. Do you know if you are getting the value you would like from the program?

Let's talk some more about employee of the month programs, as an example. There are some questions we might ask about these programs. What is the reward for being the employee of the month? Is the reward something the winner will value and feel is a fair compensation for whatever they did to be selected? How do we know? What did they do to get selected? Does what they did, or do, drive key business results? Who did the selecting, how and why? How did we announce the program? How do we know that everyone understands how it works?

We talked earlier about the importance of tying recognition and reward programs to business goals. There is no sense having these programs if they don't have some underlying positive business objective. I am assuming that point was made earlier and perhaps anyone reading this book always does that anyway. There are some other questions that need to be asked before we design and implement recognition and reward programs. Let's stay with the employee of the month concept for a little while.

If you were considering an employee of the month program, wouldn't it be a good idea to talk with some employees before you decide to go forward with it? I believe it would, and you might learn some surprising things. For starters, you are likely to learn whether the representative employee group you talk with thinks it is even worth doing. Wouldn't it be great to have a good sense whether something is going to work before you do it? You clearly try to do that with many of your other decisions, so why not this one? There is a good chance that by engaging the employee group at this early point you will get plenty of feedback about your other questions as well. In fact, are there any of the questions posed above that the employee group couldn't provide valuable input about? There is nothing quite as good as getting direct feedback from the people who will be affected before you design the program.

By engaging an employee group in the discussion about a particular type of program you might also answer another question that always comes up. Are we going to have the same winner each month, or are we going to run out of winners and have repeats? Both of these possibilities can create big issues that will likely cause more disengagement than engagement and need to be sorted out before a program is even introduced.

Does It Work For Me?

Another point for you to think about is, can you make the reward, and/or recognition fit the individual? You and I are possibly motivated by different things. You may like public recognition, and I may not. I may like a plaque, and you may like a letter. Is there any reason that recognition programs can't be very focused on the individual winners likes and dislikes? I believe there is no reason other than our lack of knowledge of the individual or our lack of willingness to learn what motivates each of our employees. I know this may sound like a daunting task if you have thousands of employees. Your organization is more than likely structured so that you have a somewhat limited number of employees that report to any one management person. I don't know whether this number would be 10 or less or up to 30 or 40 people, but in either case it is a manageable number of people to learn a bit about. Is the value of being able to design recognition and reward programs that fit the individual worth the time and effort? Once again, the Gallup Organization has done the research to help answer the question. Research of 10,000 work groups in 30 industries shows that recognition programs tailored to the preferences of the employees are the most effective. Recognition needs to be individualized, specific, and it needs to be deserved.

If you can afford to spend money to reward and recognize your employees, then make the extra effort to find out what kind of recognition or reward will have the most impact to each employee. Why go halfway and get half the impact when for a little extra effort you can multiply the impact?

The point of all this is that it is well worth your time to think clearly about what you do about answering the question of WIFM thoroughly and clearly.

Now more bits and pieces for you

What's in it for you? Does there need to be something in it for you? I suspect there does but it's a bit hard to figure out. What recognition and rewards do you want out of life? What do you think you should have or expect or deserve? Is there always something in it for you and does there need to be? I believe that if you have done a good job of thinking through what your goals are, you may have already defined what's going to be in it for you. Go back and look at your goals and think through what's in it for you.

STEP 6.

Where are my tools?

Impact of the Manager

What is management anyway? The simplest definition of management that I have ever seen is:

Management is the things you do to get things done, through others, to achieve organizational goals.

So what does that definition have to do with "where are my tools?" I believe it has everything to do with it. Although all managers do many things, isn't their primary job to assure that their team has the tools necessary to perform at their best?

When I say tools, I mean all of the different kinds of tools. There are many physical tools like offices, computers, supplies, vehicles, desks, safety equipment, telecommunication equipment and others. There are also many other kinds of tools, including information. What about training on how to do the job? What about the requirements of the job and a job description if appropriate? What about manpower? What about the climate that is created by the manager, particularly the immediate boss? What about support from the manager? All of the stuff we have been talking about up to now is the responsibility of the manager. Yes, I am using the word manager to mean anybody who is a member of the management team that has responsibility for getting things done through people, including the business owner.

Welcome Aboard

Think about the following scenario, in terms of providing tools. You have just been hired as a new member of XYZ Company. You are a trained, skilled technician and will be responsible for a key project. You have been recruited by XYZ for some time and finally decided it was the right time to make a change. You have been impressed during the recruiting process by what you could learn, you like the people you met and you are excited about getting started.

You have your start date and have been told where to be and at what time. You show up at the appointed time at the designated location. You introduce yourself to the receptionist, and he doesn't seem to have your name and calls someone to try to find out what to do with you. After a few calls he finds someone who knows your name and instructs the receptionist to send you to human resources.

You find your way to HR, and someone finally comes out and instructs you to go to a particular cubicle and indicates that they will get you some forms to complete. Now, what is going through your mind? Perhaps some thoughts like, "Didn't they know I was coming?" and "I wonder how critical the project I am going to be working on really is and how important my contribution is really going to be?" You finish your paperwork and they call your new boss to get you going. Unfortunately, your new boss has gone to lunch and everybody in HR is really busy. They suggest that you go find some lunch and check back with them in an hour or so. You go find somewhere to eat and come back and find that your new boss is back, and she asks someone in HR to walk you over to her office. As you would expect, she welcomes you and apologizes for the in-processing so far. She has a little bad news, it seems that your office isn't ready and someone forgot to order your computer.

I don't think I need to go any further with this story. Perhaps this hasn't happened to you and hopefully you haven't let it happen to anybody else. It does happen more than you might think. What message does a situation like this send to a new member of the team? Does it make them feel welcome and valued? Does it get them off to a good start? How does it make them feel about you, the new boss? Isn't this example part of providing the tools? I think it is, and I suspect you agree with me, particularly if something like this has happened to you. This is even more than only about providing tools, it's just common courtesy, or caring about how another human being feels. All of this can be overcome in the official orientation. I wonder how many companies have an organized, official orientation, and I wonder how it goes?

There Are All Kinds of Tools

MANPOWER

One of the key tools most management subordinates need is the right number of people with the right skill sets to work for them and help them achieve their goals and the goals of the company in their area of responsibility. As a boss, how do you do at providing the necessary manpower, of the right quality, to allow your subordinate team to be successful? Many industries have manpower models of some kind. These may be formal models, managed by a central manpower planning group, or nothing more than rules of thumb, or just the way it's always been done. At the end of the day, it doesn't really matter what the process is, it's important that whatever methodology used produces the necessary manpower to support the manager in the achievement of the business objectives for which he or she is responsible.

You may want to ask yourself if you are providing the appropriate manpower to allow your subordinates to be successful. Another related consideration is the impact felt by the front-line people, those actually doing the job. If they do or don't have the necessary people to do the job, it will make a big difference in how they feel about their boss and the company in general, and perhaps how they treat customers.

I have had the pleasure of leading all kinds of groups, in all kinds of circumstances, using a variety of approaches, to try to get the manpower right. If you are leading a front-line operating group, you have probably noticed that the models are more sophisticated than if you are managing a staff group of some kind. If you are leading a front-line group, in most cases, the number of people needed will be driven by the nature and timing of the work input. For example, no matter how slow the restaurant is, you will always need at least one person. No mater how full or empty an airplane is, you will always need someone on the ground to park it. If parts are coming down an assembly line, you will always need someone to assemble them. Minimums get a bit less clear as other variables are added. How many servers do you need, at what level of business, in what restaurant? How many people do you need to get the passengers, luggage and freight off the airplane, and get the outbound load on, to get it turned around fast enough to keep the airline running on time? What pace does the material flow down the production line and what are the variables? Every industry, with a front-line production or service delivery process, has some way to allocate manpower. The question is, how is the model used? If you are a manager, no matter where you work or what you do, you need a certain amount of people to get the job done.

I'm familiar with scenarios that go something like this. There is an approved, accepted manpower model, so during whatever planning horizon is in place the model is run. It may be done in an automated system or manually and could be done at a variety of different levels in different companies. The results generate the number of people needed to do the job at the required level. It would seem that this would be the end of it, a done deal. Not a chance. Now it's time for someone or some other department to second guess the results generated by the model. Are the questions ever related to adding more people than the model requires or are they always about adding less? My experience is that they are always about less. So let's say, after a debate with the boss, the decision is made that the job can be done with 10-percent less people than the model indicates and you are told, "Just figure it out." So you go figure it out knowing that on a perfect day, when everyone shows up, all the equipment is working, and the stars are aligned, and everyone is engaged, you will make it with only slightly substandard performance. But wait, finance got a look at the result and the manpower levels you and your boss agreed to will not work with the financial projections that finance had given to the CEO some time ago so the headcount is slashed another 15 percent by finance.

Are you wondering how this could happen? It happens all the time. When you look at this closely and ask yourself, who has skin in the game, what is the answer? You clearly have skin in the game and so do the front-line folks who are trying to deliver the service or product. How about your boss? Maybe, but not as much as you. How about finance? Their skin in the game is only about the numbers, so they have totally different skin in the game than you. Run this scenario a few times and what happens to engagement? The front-line, where the rubber meets the road, will give up and get into the mode of doing what they are told, missing work when they can, providing substandard service and thinking management is nuts. The message sent is management doesn't care about you, the manager, your team or the customer.

This scenario plays out in other parts of this type of organization as well. There may not be specific models, but the assumption can become we can always do more with less people, and do it with no additional tools. I have noticed that this doesn't happen much in the finance department. What staffing model does finance use and who is holding them accountable? In reality, the people who work in the finance organization make a tremendous contribution, and what they do is measurable. The challenge is that sometimes staff groups look outside for improvements and fail to look internally. If you are part of a finance organization, or any other staff group, everything in this book also applies to you, and if you implement these tools you will look great.

If you don't have the right number and kind of people in the right jobs, you will ALWAYS produce sub par results. If this happens to you, beat doors down to get it stopped and if you are doing it, stop it immediately, you are creating a slow death for your company.

PHYSICAL TOOLS

We could spend all day listing all the tools different people might need to do their jobs effectively. We aren't going to do that. It is, though, useful to have a brief conversation. This concept is pretty easy to understand. All you need to do is think about those times when you are trying to get something done and don't have the right tool. Whether you are a handy man or not, if you are trying to change or install a light at home and you don't have a ladder, or the one you have is to short, you will not get a successful result.

Take that thought out to the work place. Let's say you are working at a restaurant as a server and you are short of trays. You may be able to grab one for yourself this time but perhaps not on the next trip to the kitchen. You may find a way to make it work and get through the shift, and let's say that because of who you are, the customers don't notice and all is well. You leave that shift frustrated, but think it will be solved tomorrow night, so you forget it. It happens again the next night and you ask the boss what's going on, and get some quick, glib answer. Now how are you feeling when you go home? How many of these little tool-related issues need to happen before an employee begins to get in the mode of not caring, customers begin to suffer and your reputation, as a place to work, begins to suffer and on and on? I won't attempt to answer that question, but once is probably too many, and anything beyond once certainly is. Don't fail to provide the tools necessary to do the job, the cost is too high in many areas, JUST DON'T DO IT.

IS THE RELATIONSHIP IMPORTANT?

Perhaps another tool the boss provides is the quality of the relationship she or he has with the workforce. Is that a tool? I believe that if it helps you get your job done, it is a tool. There are many people who believe that if you don't like your boss, you won't like your job either.

One of the biggest factors in employee job satisfaction and engagement is one's relationship with the boss. In a poll by Maritz Inc., only one out of five employees is satisfied with the way the company's management relates to them. Maritz goes on to say that of the 21 percent who were satisfied, two out of three were interested in spending their entire career with the company. As times change, the likelihood of spending an entire career with any one company becomes very unlikely, if not impossible. However, for whatever amount of time an employee is with a company, the relationship they have with their direct boss is critical to their performance.

It is sometimes difficult to stay focused on the value of creating strong and positive relationships with your team when you get so busy doing your job that you forget about your team. Failure to build positive relationships with your team is a BIG mistake. There are only three reasons why you would not want to build strong relationships with your team. They are defined in the box:

> **Why would you NOT want to have a positive relationship with your subordinates?**
>
> 1. You don't know it's important. I have provided at least some information that says that it is not only important but critical. There is a good deal more research on the topic.
>
> 2. You don't care enough to want to create strong relationships. Perhaps you should be in a different job where caring is not important.
>
> 3. You don't know how to do it. Perhaps this is a plausible reason, but is it really? I assume you have positive relationships in the rest of your life, why not at work? Is it because work is different and you have to be a different person at work? If that is what you are thinking, I believe you are missing a big opportunity to not only get more engagement, but to also enjoy your work a good deal more than you may be now.

Here are some things that you might consider doing, if you can do them with integrity:

Steps toward Positive Relationships

1. Be sure you know everyone's name.
2. Learn something new about everyone that works for you.
3. Make notes of things you learn and follow up as appropriate in the future.
4. Share your life, let people in, at least a little.
5. Say good morning, every day.
6. Share mutual work challenges.
7. Ask for and offer help.
8. Let other people win.
9. Ask lots of questions and be interested in the answers.
10. Laugh together.
11. Help the team win.
12. Share your knowledge without the expectation of anything in return.
13. Be there when team members need you, support them.

If you do these things, with sincerity, you will be a long way down the path toward building positive, productive relationships at work.

TRUST, HOW IMPORTANT IS IT?

What about the role of Trust? Is trust a tool? It is worth mentioning again that providing the tools includes everything from the physical tools to the climate, the feel of the organization, and in particular the feel of the immediate boss. In the remainder of the discussion of Step 6, I will talk about a wide range of things that affect the engagement of the workforce, and they are all tools. Providing all of the tools is the responsibility of management.

Back to trust: We live in a society where we are continually bombarded with information that could lead us to believe that we can't trust anybody. We observe actions by our business, political, religious, sports leaders, and others that make us wonder if there is trust anywhere. The more we see a lack of trust the more we want to find it and hold onto it when we do find it. If we can find a boss who we can trust we are likely to be loyal back and stick with that boss as long as it makes sense for our careers. If we are lucky enough to be part of an organization that is built on trust, we may very well be part of an organization that is outperforming its competitors, retaining its people, taking risks and entering new markets, developing new products, and creating great customer loyalty. There is no doubt that trust is a valuable commodity within an organization. Trust is also one of those things that is hard to develop and easy to lose. As a manager, you must be continually aware of how your behavior impacts trust in the workplace.

What does lack of trust do to an organization? Lack of trust generates FEAR (false expectations appearing real), and fear causes people to pull into their shell. There are many different kinds of fear generated by lack of trust, including fear of rejection, loss of face, failure, some kind of punishment or just plain old embarrassment. There are plenty more but just these are devastating to the organizational climate. People want to be productive, but if they are in an environment where there is little or no trust, all but the most courageous will take steps to protect themselves from risk. The desire to contribute is always balanced against our instincts to protect ourselves. Why not create a climate where the balance is skewed toward workforce engagement and maximizing human potential? You might be surprised at who wants to contribute more.

If you agree that a trust-based environment is important and take the steps to get there, you will reap a variety of benefits, some of the steps are listed in the box on the next page.

To create an environment of trust you must do the things listed in the box and many more. The most important thing you must do is to actually mean it. Trust is developed mostly during face-to-face two-way communication. Do you believe it's possible to create an environment of trust and be a micro-manager? I know it's not. If you are going to delegate, and you must to be effective, then truly delegate and give your

Steps for Building Trust

1. Information will be shared freely.
2. Information will not be used as power and withheld; it will be shared for mutual gain.
3. Diversity and differences of opinions will be welcomed and encouraged.
4. Healthy debate will be appreciated and used to get to the best answer.
5. Everyone will be appreciated for their contribution.
6. Expectations will be clear and crisp. There will be no ambiguity about what is expected and disagreements can be discussed and resolved.
7. Commitments made will be commitments kept.
8. Ownership of issues will be the norm.
9. The messenger will not be shot; bad news will be dealt with in a positive way.
10. Management's words will be believable.
11. Communication will be open and go in both directions easily.
12. The environment will be predictable.

subordinates the room to be successful. Don't abdicate, but don't micro-manage, it will destroy an atmosphere of trust.

I would go as far as to say that you cannot achieve sustained excellence without a trusting environment. Without trust there will be no risk-taking, everybody will be covering their backsides.

It is impossible to reach out and grab the future when your hands are covering your butt.

Where does trust start? It starts at the top. Do you believe that if you are working in an environment that is not trust based that you can create trust in your particular area? I believe you can but it will only go so far. If you are working in an environment that is not trust based, I suggest you leave and go find a different environment. If you can't make the change, and you must stay, do everything possible to try to change the environment and assure that you don't get converted; your team is watching you.

THE TOOLS OF CLARITY

What other tools can you bring to the table to give yourself a shot at having an environment of full engagement? The answer to this question is to create what we have been talking about from the beginning of the book. Help your team answer the key questions that must be answered to achieve full engagement.

Acheiving an Environment of Full Engagement

1. Who are we, what do we do, where are we going? (Values, Mission, Vision)
2. What's the plan? (Strategy)
3. What do you want from me and where do I fit? (Goal Setting and Line of Sight)
4. How do I know how I am doing? (Performance Feedback)
5. What's in it for me, WIFM? (Recognition and Rewards)
6. We are on this step now.
7. How do I learn, grow and progress? (Development)

Have you effectively answered all of these questions for your team? If you have answered all of them in the affirmative, you are a rare person and/or you are in a rare organization. I hope you have answered all of them affirmatively and are in a rare organization.

Before you read any further, take a break and go out into your operation and have a conversation with some of your people and see if they are clear about all of the things in the box above. This will be a particularly interesting exercise if you have a couple layers of management below you. Go to the lowest level of management in your organization and ask them directly and then ask them to articulate the answers, not just with a yes or no. Now go to the front-line where the real rubber meets the road and ask them. What did you learn?

I hope you are happy with the results of your small survey. If you are not happy with the answers you have work to do. It is challenging work to get these questions answered clearly at every level throughout the organization and maintain that clarity, but it is worth your time to work on it until you do.

HOW WELL DO YOU KNOW YOUR TEAM?

There are a great many things that you, as a manager, can do to provide the tools your team needs to be engaged. I'm sure it is obvious that to get engagement you must be engaged. One of the easiest ways to be engaged is to care enough to really know your subordinates. How can you provide tools if you don't know your team well enough to understand what tools they need? Do you know your team members, or do you just know their names? I don't have the statistics that would tell me how well the typical manager, at any level, knows their team. My speculation, based on my long exposure to managers at all levels, is that most managers don't know their subordinates very well. By very well, I mean knowing what turns them on and off. What they like and don't like. What's going on in their lives outside work that could impact their work performance? Do they really understand what they are doing and the impact it has on the overall organization? How do they feel about you really? What kind of recognition is most meaningful to them, not you? Are you engaged enough or care enough to know them better?

There are a variety of ways to get to know the team better, the easiest and most effective is to ask questions. Why not just be straightforward and ask; how bad can it be? You might actually learn something that will really help you understand what makes them tick. You can also use assessments to learn more. There are assessments for nearly everything, from learning more about personalities, to learning how your key players are viewed by each other, their bosses and their subordinates. You could also just pay attention, and I mean real attention. By whatever means, it will be useful for you to know as much as possible about your team so you can manage them as individuals, not just as headcount, full-time equivalents or some other term.

HOW WELL DO YOU COMMUNICATE?

As a manager, how do you communicate? I know you have many tools such as emails, memos, social media, intranets, meetings, conversations and more. But I'm asking how you really communicate? How much of your communication is about asking questions and listening versus talking? Your impact on your team from listening will be much stronger than when you are talking. Think of the benefits of asking questions and listening. You can add to the list, but in the box are a few of them:

The Value of Listening and Asking Questions

- You present as interested.
- You appear to care about whatever the topic is.
- You may have the opportunity to gather some new information.
- You put the person you are talking with in the position of being able to communicate in his or her own way.
- You can probe and reframe questions in a way to get more and more information.
- You may give the other person the opportunity to get something off his or her chest, and that something may be valuable to you.
- You usually have to be out in the work environment, out of your office, to ask questions and listen.
- While you are out asking questions and listening, you also have the opportunity to observe other things.
- You can provide the other person with the opportunity to take the lead.
- Listen fully as opposed to developing your answer, the person you are communicating with will know. We listen at a great deal faster pace than we talk, so you won't fall behind by listening.

There are many more benefits from asking questions and listening, and I encourage you to think about them and give them the weight they deserve.

You may also want to think about the way you ask questions and how you respond to the answers. One of the big demotivators to any person you are communicating with is the famous "but eraser." Think about the times when you have shared an idea with someone or made a suggestion and they said "yes, but." I suspect that it's likely that whatever you said before the "yes, but" felt erased by the other person's "but." I know it feels that way to me. If you feel like there is something else to be added in those situations, I suggest that you either save it until later or use a "yes, and" approach. I know this sounds like a small deal, but it's not. The next time the "yes, but" is done to you when you think you have something valuable to add, you will feel the eraser, and it won't feel good.

You should also think about how you ask questions. Think about the words you use and the tone of your voice, both things will impact the answer you get. It is important to present as open and interested, as opposed to aggressive and in-their-face. Avoid being accusatory in your tone of questioning. Be careful how you ask "why?" as it is an inflammatory question most of the time. Find a better way to find out why, such as "tell me more." If you really want to learn something ask open-ended questions, those questions that can't be answered with a simple yes or no. You will be surprised how much you can learn by simply opening the door, and open-ended questions do that for you.

Another great opportunity for communication is meetings. If you have been managing for a while, you are probably rolling your eyes and trying to remember the last productive meeting you attended. Think about the meetings you have attended and why they were or were not productive. For starters, meetings should not be held unless they are the most productive and cost effective way to resolve an issue, get to a result, disseminate information, etc. If this standard was applied across the board there would be a lot less meetings and millions of saved man-hours and dollars.

In the box on the next page are a few things to think about before you schedule a meeting. You may want to share these things with other members of your organization who schedule meetings.

After the meeting, gather the meeting notes and distribute a memo to all attendees. If appropriate, copy other people who will be interested in or impacted by decisions made at the meeting. Assure that all

Meeting Tips

1. Ask yourself if you really need to have a meeting.
2. Clarify the objective of the meeting and include it in the agenda.
3. Decide what kind of a meeting it is going to be. It's not particularly productive to mix meetings that are going to be focused on creative issues, using brainstorming as a methodology, with meetings that are more analytical in nature.
4. Decide who needs to be at the meeting based on the purpose of the meeting. Invite only those people who are needed.
5. Set a definite date and start and finish time. Determine in advance that the scheduled time will work for the people who you need in attendance.
6. Produce and distribute an agenda well in advance of the meeting, including clarifying any responsibilities of the attendees.
7. Let everyone know who will be attending the meeting.
8. Organize all the administrative details, such as securing the room, having any needed A/V equipment and supplies, the right number of chairs, refreshments when needed, etc.
9. Always make provision for someone to take good notes.
10. Start the meeting on time. One of the largest wastes of management time is driven by meetings that don't start on time.
11. Clarify any responsibilities that come out of the meeting

agreements at the meeting are clearly and accurately documented in the meeting notes to create action and accountability. Distribute the memo to everyone involved in the meeting. Although there are questions you could ask yourself after the meeting to determine whether it was a success or not, I suggest that you ask only one question: Was the objective of the meeting met? If you have written a clear objective and it was met, chances are that the meeting was productive and successful.

DO YOU DELEGATE OR ABDICATE, OR NEITHER?

Have you thought about the above question? If you haven't, you should think about it now. Delegating is giving someone else the responsibility and authority to get a task done, while staying connected to the person, and the task, to assure that they are able to complete it. Remember that you still have the ultimate responsibility for the task. You don't just get to pass it on and skate. Abdicating is giving someone the authority and responsibility for a task, and then forgetting about it and not following up at all. Remember you are still accountable. If the task is not completed when it is required, at the required quality level, you have a problem. How can you possibly get things done through others (remember the definition of management) without delegating? The truth is, you can't. In addition, you are cheating your subordinate team out of the opportunity to learn and grow. If you don't ever give your subordinates the room to fail, how can they learn to succeed?

Delegation Principles

1. Be certain that the task you want to delegate is better done by someone else rather than you. This may be about time, expertise or development.

2. If you are going to delegate, assure that you delegate both the responsibility and authority.

3. Before you delegate a task, be sure that the person you are delegating to has, or can readily get, the tools to complete the task.

4. Assure that you provide clear and complete instructions related to the task, including the nature of the final product, quality level, who it is being done for, required deadlines and follow-up dates.

(continued on next page)

> ### Delegation Principles (continued)
>
> 5. Agree, up front, how often you will want to have a status report during the delegation period, and then live with it.
> 6. Don't just delegate junk, delegation isn't about getting rid of stuff, it's about getting the job done in the most effective manner, and developing people.
> 7. Be available to help if it is needed and make that point clear, up front. However, don't fall in the trap of letting the task be delegated back to you. Don't take the monkey.

Delegation is one of the areas that many managers have a hard time dealing with. Since many managers have been promoted to their management positions because they were very good at the particular jobs they are now responsible for supervising, it is sometimes difficult for them to give up the pleasure of doing the jobs themselves. If you are reading this and thinking that you are one of those managers, find a way to learn how to delegate, because until you do you will be limiting your progression. Find and read books, take classes and seminars, or just perform the steps above. Delegation is like most other things, it is much easier once you start to do it.

WRITE IT DOWN

In these days of electronic communication, it may seem strange to have someone suggest that writing something is useful to a manager. It actually is. If you are a busy manager, and who isn't, how do you stay on top of all the conversations, commitments and follow-up opportunities that happen in the line of fire? My view is that you don't, unless you write it down. Taking notes is not about covering your butt, it's about staying on top of everything and following through on your commitments. If you are managing by walking around, you are going to become engaged in conversations all over the place about all kinds of things. Many of these conversations are not going to be the conversations you had in mind.

As an example, as you are walking around, you become engaged in a conversation about the performance measurement system for a particular process. This isn't what you planned on discussing so you are not necessarily ready for it. Assuming you are really interested in feedback and input from your team, you listen with positive intent (non-judgmental, solution focused, no preconceived answers), wanting to provide real value to the team. After a robust discussion, joined by a few other teammates, you agree that they have a point and say that you will follow up. As you leave the area where the discussion took place, you get a message on your smartphone to call your boss immediately. You decide to hustle to your office where you have some files and dial the phone. When your boss answers and realizes it's you, he starts in immediately on the reason for his call. He has just received a call from your largest customer with a problem that was generated from your area of responsibility. After the discussion, and a bit of back and forth, your priorities have changed and you are focused on solving this immediate problem. This issue now has your full attention and the discussion about the performance metrics a couple hours ago is now somewhere in your subconscious, with no immediate retrieval mechanism.

A few days pass as you continue to work on the immediate and other issues, and you run into one of the teammates that engaged you in the performance metrics conversation. It takes you a while to remember the conversation, since so much has gone on since then. As you might guess, the team member has kept it at the top of her mind, since it can impact her bonus, and bonus time is getting close. You now have to find a way to recover, without losing credibility. You may be able to recover without taking a hit to your credibility or you may not. Either way, if you had taken a note about the earlier conversation and your commitment, chances are you would have been able to stay on top of it despite your other distractions. Even if the performance metrics issue had taken a back seat, you could have called one of the team members and let them know what had happened and when you would be back on top of it.

The scenario I just described happens all the time and erodes management credibility. I am assuming you believe your credibility and your response and follow up with your team is important. Your credibility is one of the tools you provide to get the full engagement of your team. Situations like this one that can severely damage credibility can be avoided by WRITING IT DOWN. I know it's old fashioned and if it's easier for you to make notes in the notes section of whatever kind of smartphone you use, be my guest, but make some kind of a note of the conversation and commitment. By doing so, you will at least have a shot at remembering it and taking the appropriate action, even when major distractions arise.

THE TOOLS OF LAUGHTER AND FUN

Is there fun in your work environment? How about laughter? If not, why not? Do you think there is some reason work has to always be serious? Think about it, what is that reason? Is it about making money, satisfying customers, taking risk, making the numbers? What is it about? Let's look at it another way. Can you achieve all of your objectives and still have fun and plenty of laughter in the workplace?

There is zero, none, zilch research that I can find that says that succeeding in business, whether in a job in a corporate environment, or running your own business, needs to be driven by a boring, humorless fun-free environment. On the other hand, there is adequate research that suggests that fun and laughter is productive. If you decide that having this kind of an environment is a good idea, guess what, the ball is in your court. Whether you are the owner, CEO, or a department manager, you can still do it. It's about deciding to. It's about deciding that work is still about life.

Why should people who like to have fun come to work and be different? The answer is, there is no reason. There is nothing that says you can't have fun and still be held accountable for achieving organizational goals, or that you can't hold others accountable. Do you think more gets done with stern faces than smiles? That thought, if you happen to have it, is B.S., so forget it. If you think there is not enough fun happening where you work, make it happen.

Creating the right environment is YOUR responsibility. Make it happen.

THE TOOLS OF LEADERSHIP

There are far too many philosophies of leadership to cover in this section. You need to read and study and arrive at your own conclusion about what you believe leadership is and how you want to demonstrate it. I will provide one suggestion that, in my view, is universal. You must know yourself. This may be the most difficult challenge in understanding what true leadership is, and you may never fully get there. If you will accept this requirement, and work on getting there for the rest of your life, you will find that your leadership skill will continue to improve as you continue in your role as a leader, in all facets of your life. If you feel cheated in this section, I apologize, but there isn't time or room to do the topic justice, and you need to arrive at your own place, not mine, or anyone else's. I will close the comments on the tools with the best definition of leadership I have ever seen, and I don't know where I saw it.

> *Leadership is "the art of mobilizing others to want to struggle for shared aspirations."*

Provide the tools and reap the benefits.

You have probably reached the conclusion that providing tools is all about you and you are responsible for all the tools. You are absolutely right. If you thought this book was going to give you an easy solution, it does. If you implement and follow the **seven steps** to an engaged workforce, you will have success, but the tools are all about you. The point is that the tools range all the way from the simplest of physical tools to the environment you create, and the ball is in your court to provide them. Please take the time to continue to learn and understand, and the more you learn, particularly about yourself, the better you will become at providing the tools needed to get the full engagement of your workforce.

Now more bits and pieces for you

You can see from this previous discussion that there are many tools needed by your workforce to support engagement and productivity. I haven't listed every possible tool, but I made the list broad enough that you get the point. You might say, "so what?" If you are saying that and providing all these tools and any others that your workforce needs that's OK. However, if not, perhaps there is a bigger problem. Whether or not you are providing all the tools goes back to your intention as a manager. Is your intention to support the success of your team? Do you believe that they come to work wanting to do a great job, be engaged and productive? Do you believe you need them more than they need you?

Your intentions drive your behavior and if you want engaged, high-performing team members, you must have the internal intention to provide them with everything they need, and do everything you can to allow them to be the best they can be. Provide all the tools and everyone wins.

STEP 7.

How do I learn, grow and progress?

Development Opportunities

The development of people is a key leadership responsibility. If you, the leader, don't take this responsibility who will? Who took the responsibility to help you? If you are thinking, "I did it all myself," I think that it is likely that you are not looking close enough, or deep enough. In the off chance that you have done it all yourself I would say that you are a very special person and you have been very fortunate. That fact doesn't relieve you of the responsibility to develop your team.

In a survey sponsored by Hewitt Associates, a global human resources services firm, and HR People+ Strategy, a panel of independent judges selected 20 U.S. companies as the best at developing leaders. Hewitt Associates conducted a study comparing the companies on the list with 350 other U.S. companies. The comparison showed that the top 20 companies realize that with the large number of baby boomers who are retiring now and will be retiring over the next while, it is critical that their leadership development efforts are strong and positive. They clearly understand that the only true way for their development goals to be met is with the full engagement of the senior leadership of the company. The next box highlights some of the practices that differentiate the top companies from the rest, according to the survey results.

> **Results achieved by companies with a strong emphasis on development:**
>
> - 85 percent of these companies hold their leaders accountable for developing their direct reports, compared with 46 percent of other companies.
> - 53 percent of the top companies earmark between 6 percent and 15 percent of incentive pay for leadership development, versus 34 percent of other companies that do so.
> - 95 percent of these companies say their leadership initiatives attract quality leaders to their organizations, compared with 59 percent of other organizations.
> - 95 percent of top companies have a CEO succession plan; less than 60 percent of other companies have one.
> - 85 percent of top companies promoted their current CEO from within, versus 68 percent of the other companies.

"The lesson learned," according to HR People+ Strategy, is that "no matter what your company size or business, an organization that offers quality leadership development programs will attract stronger leaders and will increase their chances for success in the long run."

The American Society of Training and Development (ASTD) has found that those companies with best practices in the learning function are among those with the highest levels of financial performance. ASTD found interesting correlations when looking at key measures of financial performance. For example, the firms in the top quartile of the study group, as measured by average expenditures on training per employee, enjoyed higher profit margins (by 24 percent), higher income per employee (by 218 percent) and higher price-to-book ratios (by 26 percent) on average than firms in the bottom quarter.

A group of organizations that define and share best practices in learning, have also consistently outperformed the S&P 500, by a factor of 7 during a 14-year period. A $21,000 investment in the portfolio of S&P best winners in 2000 would be worth $36,000 in 2005. And $36,000 invested in the Benchmarking Forum portfolio between 1991 and 2005 would be worth $741,652 in 2005.

At a minimum, the above statistics are very compelling.

The remainder of this step will be spent discussing development from the standpoint of those below the senior leadership of the organization.

Although attracting and retaining key senior leaders is a key issue, providing opportunities for those who are already in the organization at lower levels is critical to achieving the full engagement of the workforce. The million-dollar question is how you make this happen. The first thing you need to do is understand that it's important and actually want to do it. I have had the good fortune of participating in dozens of developmental programs over the past 35 years. These opportunities started for me immediately upon joining my first company after completing graduate school.

Like many young men and women coming out of undergraduate or graduate school, I had the pleasure of joining the training program of a major company. At that point in my career anything would have been interesting. I was given the opportunity to experience a few weeks of training that included wide exposure to various aspects of the company, and to receive training in a variety of locations. This also gave me the opportunity to meet many of my young peers from around the U.S. and the world. All of this early training was job related and gave me many tools that I was able to take advantage of throughout the rest of the time I spent with that company. This training also made me feel very good about the company I was part of. I appreciated the chance to learn and meet people, and get off to a good start with the company. Training opportunities continued throughout the time I spent with this company and I appreciated all of it, and it all added value and continued to increase my positive feelings about the company. By the way, all of that early training also provided me with a very good starter tool kit that I was able to build on throughout my career there. It helped me be a better developer of people, regardless of what resources were provided by the company.

I'm sure you are reading this and notice that I have said I was doing this or that, while I was at the company. This could lead you to believe that I didn't stay at that company for my entire career. You are correct, I didn't. I stayed there long enough to become a vice president and chief operating officer with responsibility for a $200-million revenue division. I ultimately left for the main reason many people leave a company they are enjoying.

> *An organizational change left me with*
> *a toxic boss, and I left.*

Let's go back to the questions of how to go about providing development opportunities for your team, and how do you know what to do for whom?

What you do and how you go about it will be greatly impacted by the size of your team, your personal capabilities and what the needs and opportunities are. If your company is big enough, you may have the good fortune to have a training department, with a quality leader, and you can develop training programs and implement them in-house, and tailor them to your specific needs. If you are reading this as a small business owner, more than likely you don't have the benefit of being able to afford a training department in-house. Considering that likelihood, I will spend the rest of the chapter talking about your possibilities. I will, however, make a few comments for those who are leaders in larger companies.

Even if you have the benefit of having a capable training department in your company, the responsibility for the training and development of your people is still yours. If you think about it, you will come to the conclusion that it's in your best interest anyway. Who benefits the most if you have fully trained, competent people working for you? The answer is clear, you do. In addition, if you develop a reputation as a developer the best people are going to want to work for you, so you win in a variety of ways. Let's step back and assume that you do have a good training group, and you accept the responsibility for the development of your people. What do you do? At a minimum, you can do the following things listed on the next page to support the corporate development efforts and thereby your own success:

Tips for Supporting Training and Development

- Be a visible advocate of the training and development group.
- Provide input to T&D so you get the kind of training that you know will be best for your team.
- Participate yourself by attending, introducing training and teaching.
- Discuss the training before your people attend and again when they return.
- Be sure that the leadership style you demonstrate when your team members return supports the training.
- Take the time to send the right people to the training. All training and development efforts are not for everyone.
- Make attending T&D programs a positive thing.
- Make T&D a prerequisite for promotions, special assignments and other opportunities.

These are a few of the things you can do. There are other things that can be done based on the circumstances you find yourself in. Bottom line, be a supportive, visible fan. Your behavior can make or break the effort.

You may also find yourself in a large company that could and perhaps should have a training and development organization but for some reason doesn't. The ball is still in your court. In this case you are going to have to figure out what to do and how to do it on your own. There is no reason that you can't provide training and development yourself. Depending on your level of skill, perhaps you can hold classes that you facilitate. If you don't have those skills, perhaps someone on the team does and has the interest. You certainly can provide the right example to the team by the way you behave and be sure they recognize the value of certain behaviors over others. You can share articles and books with the team. You may even want to have them read a book and have discussions to assure that the key lessons are received and understood. If you have a budget for it, you can send them to seminars from time to time. You may be able to get guest speakers to come to your staff meetings from time to time. You can retain a coach to support individual and team development. The point of all of this is that by taking these proactive steps you are demonstrating that you care, and that your team's continual development is important. You are taking the bull by the horns to do what you can to support the learning, growth and development of your team.

You will find that there are people out there who believe that, at a certain level, continual development is not important. If you can, ignore these people and make it happen anyway. There is no level after which continual development becomes unimportant. Can you ever know enough? Is there a time when you should no longer support and encourage the growth of your people? I believe not.

What if you are running a small company and don't have the resources of a training department? If you believe it is important to provide development opportunities for your people you will find a way. Here are some possible paces to look:

Training and Development Resources

- Start looking within your own company; you may have more resources and skills than you think, so ask.

- Do it yourself. If you have the interest and the skills you can provide much, if not most, of the developmental needs yourself.

- Local community colleges usually have classes on a variety of management topics, and many times, depending on the size of your need, they can do things at your location, custom made for you.

- Local universities usually have many possibilities to offer as well. They may be more costly than community colleges.

(continued on next page)

Training and Development Resources (continued)

- The American Management Association (AMA) has courses both live and online. They may have something scheduled in or near your city. Their course offerings are wide and deep.
- There are a wide variety of training companies around the country with a wide range of classes for all levels of people. Hundreds of these companies can be found by entering "management training" in Google.
- The American Society of Training and Development (ASTD) can provide a wide range of choices. They can be contacted at ASTD.com.
- The Society of Human Resource Management (SHRM) can provide access to a wide range of resources as well. They can be reached at SHRM.com.
- Major universities around the country, such as Harvard Business School, offer developmental opportunities for more senior level development, including extensive executive M.B.A. programs and other programs.
- Online provider Lynda.com has great courses.
- Online provider Mind Tools has great courses.

If you want to develop people, the resources are available. One of the decisions you will have to make is, what is it worth to you? This decision will determine how broad your search needs to be.

Now more bits and pieces for you

Unless you are continuing to learn and grow you are going backwards.

What was the last book you read before this one? When did you last attend a seminar to improve your skill, at anything? Have you attended a college class recently? What newspapers do you read daily? What magazines do you subscribe to or buy and read regularly? What organizations are you part of where you get exposed to broader viewpoints? What kind of CD's do you listen to in your car? How much time do you spend poking around on the internet, just learning? What new skill have you learned recently?

It doesn't matter what your age, you absolutely must continue to explore and learn. While I was in graduate school, a friend of mine and I opened a clothing store on our university campus as a branch of a store that was in our hometown. The store in our hometown was owned by two young men who had been out of college for only a few years. I recall one of the owners saying to me that he was proud of the fact that he had not read one book since he had finished college. I was amazed by that statement and still am. I hope you are too.

Don't ever stop learning and growing, it just may help keep you young.

We have made our way through the **seven steps** to an engaged, productive workforce. Now what?

I am hopeful that you have picked up a few pointers that you can use, or at least, have had your good thinking reinforced. The intent of this book has been to give you some tools you can immediately use. I encourage you to review and take advantage of the list of books and resources included in the back of the book.

The bottom line of this book is, IT'S ALL ABOUT YOU. As a leader, no matter what your title, the responsibility for providing the environment that will facilitate the engagement of your workforce is yours.

Summary, Review and Recommendations for Leaders

As I have been writing this book, I am troubled by the fact that the workforce engagement level in the U.S., as measured by Gallup, has stagnated at around 30 percent for over 15 years. I am even more concerned because I believe it is possible that 30 percent of the workforce is naturally engaged, in spite of their work environment or boss, and that might mean that there has been no impact at all from all the engagement initiatives. I have discussed this possibility with a variety of my colleagues and they are inclined to agree, since in their careers they have always been engaged in spite of their work environment and/or boss, as have I. If we have been unable to get the environment we wanted at various stages in our careers, we managed to maneuver into a different internal environment or we left the company for a more appropriate opportunity. We are intrinsically motivated and I believe it's possible that people like us make up the 30 percent of the workforce today.

Does my conversation above mean that I have wasted my time writing this book and you have wasted your time reading it? I don't think so in either case. Remember that the Gallup research also shows that only about 40 percent of managers, executives and officers are engaged. Perhaps we as leaders at various levels just need to take more accountability and personal initiative for helping our co-workers become more engaged. I believe this will require more real concern and caring by anyone with a management or leadership responsibility, at a time when the pace of everything is accelerating. As leaders it is all about our intention toward our team members (the workforce).

I am encouraged by the initiative between Gallup and McKinsey that I mentioned in the introduction. Two well-known and respected large organizations teaming up to make a difference in the productivity of organizations throughout the world is exciting. I applaud their effort and I'm hopeful that the contribution of this book will also make a positive impact one leader and one organization at a time.

The workplace is becoming more interesting and complex, driven by rapid changes in technology. These changes have generated book after book and article after article about workforce groupings such as millennials, Gen X, baby boomers and traditionalists and the different ways they are believed to work. We have always had generational variations in the workforce, but technology is clearly highlighting the differences more now than ever.

In spite of the changes that are happening everywhere, including in the workplace, people are still people. Now more than ever as leaders we are all going to need to spend more time understanding human behavior and supporting the success of our multi-generational workforce in achieving both their and our goals. To do that we must have the intention of understanding our team members enough to provide the tools for our mutual success.

So Now What?

The only way to get a return on the time you have spent reading the book is to decide that your team requires more than ever from you and that you are willing to make the personal investment for their success and yours. This section will go back through all the **seven steps** for creating an engaged, productive workforce and offer some summary comments and advice for actions you can take right now.

Step 1. Who are we, what do we do, where are we going?
(Purpose, Values, Mission and Vision).

It is important for your workforce to know the rules of the road. What are the things we always and never do around here? How do we behave? How do we treat each other? What's acceptable and what isn't? It is also important for them to know, with as much clarity as possible, what the company does and where is it headed. What is the purpose behind the company? WHAT IS YOUR CATHEDRAL?

You should spend as much time as necessary to define a purpose that is bigger than just the products or services your company provides. Your workforce wants to be proud of what they do and think that it's important. Chances are, what you do has a bigger purpose than most people, including you, have considered. I know that if you are a business owner your profit and loss is critical. I know that if you are a leader in someone else's company you are interested in your career as well as the bottom-line success of the company. I also know that if you want to maximize your success you need an engaged workforce and they need to understand the higher purpose of the company. Define your cathedral.

Start right now. Take the time to define and describe your version of the cathedral. Help your workforce find it as well by engaging them in the search, or at least the understanding of your version of the cathedral. Get passionate about it yourself and they may join you. Nothing that has been discussed in this book is going to get done if you don't get it started and make it happen with your team. It's a down-in-the-trenches, gloves-off kind of effort and you will need to take the initiative and stay engaged to make it happen.

Hold individual and team meetings. Ask questions and listen to the answers.

Employees want to be involved, so open the opportunity for them and thank them when they respond. They want to be proud of their company and what it does. Help them. Get to really know them and what drives their pride, commitment and engagement. As leaders we are all in the people business, and the price of entry into today's engagement game is to truly care and provide opportunities for all team members to actively participate. They want to make a difference, so open the opportunities for them.

Step 2. What's the plan?
(Strategy and Corporate Goals)

It is important to define your version of the cathedral, but what's the plan for building it. Your team wants to know. If there isn't a plan, how will you and they know what steps to take and in what order and in what direction? How many wrong turns will you take and wrong roads will you travel down? How can you get everyone going in the same direction if you don't let them know where they are headed and why they are going there?

Strategic planning is a broad field and much has been written about it. The approach you take is up to you, but you need to have a strategy and the workforce needs to know what it is. I believe the best way to get from where you are to where you are going is to start where you are. Be sure you know where you are and make sure your team knows as well.

Do a SWOT analysis to be clear about where you are. Involve all of the necessary team members and encourage them to be open and provide their true viewpoints.

Once you have developed a strategy, either with your internal team or with outside help, be sure that the strategy is understood up and down the organization. You can never get anyone engaged and enthusiastic about something they don't know exists, or that they don't understand clearly. Give your team the benefit of the doubt and involve them in the development of the strategy. Make a 1000-percent effort to assure that they are clear about where you are going. Involvement and clarity support engagement and commitment. The strategy has to come to life with your corporate goals. What do you want to achieve in the next period to maximize your strategy, how will you measure success and how will it impact each of your team members?

Step 3. What do you want from me and where do I fit? (Goal Setting and Alignment)

Although I believe each of the **seven steps** toward the full engagement of your workforce provides valuable resources, this is the one that you cannot do without.

How in the world can you expect anyone to get where they are going, or know when they have arrived if they don't have a destination in mind? Well, on second thought, perhaps they can get where THEY are headed, or at least end up somewhere, but not where you want them to end up. There is a key difference.

As you probably know, the late Peter Drucker provided some very early insight about the value of having goals that are clear and aligned from the top to the bottom of any business enterprise or business unit. His introduction of the concept of management by objectives (MBO), offered an organized way for business leaders to think about how they might align their teams around common goals. Although Peter Drucker, who lived to be 95 years old, introduced the MBO concept very long ago and introduced many, many insightful concepts, I believe this was one of his most powerful.

People want to feel engaged in something. Most people spend more of their waking hours at work than anywhere else. There is no doubt that providing people with the opportunity to understand what the company they are working for is trying to achieve, where they fit, how they can make a difference and what's in it for them is a basic requirement to achieve engagement and productive results.

As you are going through the goal-setting process, be sure that you are fully engaging all employees in the setting of their goals and don't set them for them. They are much more likely to feel good and committed to their goals if they feel that they have been fully involved in developing them, and if they understand how they help the company achieve the overall goals. Your next challenge is establishing high clarity up and down the organization. All of the goals in the organization must be aligned and each person must fully understand how what they do supports the overall goals of the company and feel positive about it.

One of the challenges leaders/managers face in implementing a solid goal setting, tracking and feedback system that helps align the organization, is how to cascade the goals down through the organization. I would suggest that when beginning the goal setting task you think this process through completely, and assure that every individual member of your team is on board and knows how to translate the goals from one level to the next. The process needs to not only assure alignment but also engagement and commitment at every step of the way. Commitment can only be achieved by authentic involvement starting with the leader.

Don't be clear and specific only with the senior level in the organization and then expect them to do the rest. You must personally stay involved with goal setting and alignment throughout the entire process, from your direct reports to the newest front-line employee. You will also need to test to see if you have been successful. When goals have been agreed upon by front-line employees, ask them how achieving their goals will support the success of the company. If they can't answer that question to your satisfaction, you have not been successful in creating the alignment required for full engagement and you need to take the necessary steps right then to create clarity.

When you have completed the goal-setting process from top to bottom and assured that there is alignment and understanding, you have a couple more steps. You must be sure that each goal can be measured in a way that is clear and that the person being measured understands and agrees with. They also must be able to clearly identify how their performance impacts the overall success of the organization. If the measurement process is not clearly understood and fair your entire process will come apart. This is true for every goal at every level.

The additional step that you must take is requiring each team member to have action plans supporting the achievement of each of their goals. I have had disappointing experiences when I have allowed my team to talk me out of the need for this step. Experienced managers may be inclined to tell you that they will just make it happen and that they don't need to do the action plans. They may be correct in saying this, or perhaps not. It's just logical to believe that if you have a goal that has steps that need to be taken toward reaching it, that those steps should be thought through and recorded so progress can be tracked to support goal achievement. It may take additional time to work with team members to help them establish action plans, but it will be worth the effort. Do not skip this step.

Spend the time necessary to get goal setting, alignment, measuring, planning and tracking right and fully involve the team in the process. This investment will pay off big time for you and failing to do it can completely derail any effort to engage your team.

Step 4. How do I know how I am doing?
(Performance Feedback)

If you get the goal setting right and then don't let people know how they are doing you are very likely to get off track. Without appropriate and timely feedback people will keep doing what they are comfortable with doing or what they think they should be doing to achieve the goals you have agreed on. That process may or may not result in achieving what was agreed.

Frequent feedback is critical. The method for providing feedback is also very important to the impact it will have on the person receiving it. Regular and current real-time feedback is important. If you have designed the goals and measurement systems correctly there may be good feedback coming through naturally from the job itself and regular conversations that happen in the natural course of the business. Even so, you need to recognize and comment on successes as appropriate. Don't forget the value of the regular thank you. Don't forget to provide detailed and specific recognition for exceptional work. Get to know each team member well enough to be able to recognize them in the manner that they appreciate most. In addition to this day-to-day feedback, I strongly recommend that you establish a process of providing formal written performance feedback and discussions at least once a quarter. Formal feedback should have the elements in the box, as a minimum:

Requirements for Successful Formal Feedback

1. Schedule the feedback meeting far enough out that preparation is possible.
2. Allot enough time to allow for a thorough, two-way, open and positive discussion.
3. Hold the meeting in an environment of no interruptions.
4. Hold it with the intention of achieving clarity.
5. Document the meeting results so that both parties are clear about the status and required next steps, if any.
6. Emphasize to participants that they must come prepared.
7. Focus on objective results.
8. Use the meeting as an opportunity to celebrate success and also to course correct if necessary.
9. Have a positive focus during the meeting.
10. Make it personally tailored to the person you are meeting with.

If a performance review is held at least quarterly, and has at least the elements described above, it will facilitate not only the achievement of the agreed goals, but also the communication between the person being reviewed and the reviewer. If you do this and do it well, you will find that these quarterly reviews will result in good, solid and in-depth conversations about what is really happening in your organization and with the individual being reviewed.

Remember that the team members out there dealing with issues and serving customers, both internal and external, have a better view of reality than you do. Although you hold various meetings during the quarter and provide day-to-day feedback, don't underestimate the value of a formal sit-down review with each team member each quarter. It just feels different and it gives an additional measure of credibility. Don't miss these quarterly review opportunities.

Step 5. What's in it for me ... WIFM?
(Recognition, Rewards, Appreciation and Feeling Successful)

Remember that in designing any system of rewards and recognition, you must get the basics correct. Every member of your team expects to be treated fairly.

In the area of base compensation, this means fairness relative to similar positions outside your company as well as relative positions within. This also applies to your benefit programs. You can't be out of whack with your competition and expect to attract and keep the best people. As Dan Pink, author of "Drive" says, "Make your compensation competitive and fair so you take the topic of money off the table."

There are many places you can go to get feedback on compensation and benefits. I suggest that you take the time to assure that you are at least at parity. Don't overlook the opportunity to create additional engagement by offering some form of gain-sharing designed to be supportive of your culture of engagement. Before you decide to implement any form of incentive compensation be sure that it is really going to be motivational as opposed to becoming just the opposite, and having a negative impact. I have mentioned Dan Pink a few times and suggest that you read his book "Drive" or attend a webinar or his TED Talk and understand what the research says about incentives.

There are many ways to share your success and recognize those that support you. The options range from profit sharing, stock options, stock gifts and on and on. If you decide to introduce one or more of these options, be sure that everyone clearly understands the program and the effect it will have on them.

Beyond the basic compensation and benefits and gain-sharing programs the opportunities are wide open for how creative you want to be in rewarding and recognizing your team. Remember—many forms of recognition are FREE.

Don't overlook the value of THANK YOU. It is free and not heard enough in business today. Keep in mind that the more appropriate the form of recognition is to the things that are valued by the people being recognized, the more impactful it will be for them. Know your people's interests. Be sure that your recognition and reward programs support your company's objectives. Don't do something just because you have heard other companies have done it. The employee of the month is one of those programs that is widely used and is often unproductive. Talk with your team; engage them in defining what will turn them on. Just think clearly about how you would like to be recognized or rewarded, but instead of doing that recognize it's not about you, it's about your team and the individual members. Remember if you are going to recognize a team member, or the entire team for doing a great job, get specific. What specifically did they do, how important was it and what was the positive result generated? And how proud are you of them?

Step 6. Where are my tools?
(Impact of the Manager)

We have spent a great deal of time on this topic. I can't emphasize enough, that you, the manager, make all the difference in the world. You set the tone, control the information flow, provide the physical tools, organize the training, create the climate, generate the trust, allocate the manpower, and much more. We have talked about all of these things earlier. The manager is responsible for making it happen. Remember the two earlier definitions of management and leadership.

Management is: "The things you do to get things done through others to achieve organizational goals."

Leadership is: "The art of mobilizing others to want to struggle for shared aspirations."

As the manager you are responsible. I'm sure you have heard the statement: "People join companies and leave managers." You are the person the team looks up to. You need to be aware that every move you make and word you say has a stronger impact on team members than anyone else, and much stronger than you may believe. Everything that you say and do is noticed, amplified and has a higher impact than what anyone else says or does. It may not be fair but it is true that you are held to a higher standard. You are the person who must always be clear, always willing to listen, always compassionate, always supportive, always concerned about the whole person, always willing to take action when there is inadequate performance and so on.

The manager must have broad shoulders. You must understand how to achieve the balance between being confident and strong, but also vulnerable, so you are seen as a real person. You must be emotionally aware. You must be the trainer and developer. You must be the strategic planner and the idea guy or gal and still encourage every team member to be involved and interested in the overall company.

Don't underestimate your personal impact. Provide the tools and take advantage of every opportunity to listen, encourage and engage every member of your team. It will pay big dividends.

Step 7. How do I learn, grow and progress? (Development Opportunities)

It is the responsibility of the manager to provide the opportunity for team members to learn and grow. With the coming shortage in many kinds of skilled workers, it will become increasingly more important for companies to provide a learning environment. Whether you are part of a very large company, with vast resources, or a small business owner, the requirement will be the same. Even if you are a middle manager in a large company, the degree to which you find creative ways to help your team learn and grow will set you apart and give you an advantage in attracting, retaining and engaging the most talented people.

Make yourself familiar with all of the resources that are available to help your team learn and grow. Be a resource yourself. Continually read and research. Join progressive industry organizations. Pay attention to what is going on in education and corporate training. Attend seminars yourself. Use the internet to do research. There are abundant free resources. Become familiar with the current assessments on the market; they may be very valuable in helping you make hiring decisions and also give you a bit of a look under the hood that you may not have without taking advantage of some of these tools. There are newsletters, articles, white papers and studies of all kinds. Join or be sure that someone in your organization joins SHRM and ASTD. Stay on top of what is happening; it will give you an edge. Get acquainted with the key people at your local community colleges and universities. Be interested and inquisitive about how you can provide a stronger learning environment and you may learn something you can apply as well.

Today's workforce expects you to provide opportunities for them to learn and grow. Find out early what their expectations really are and meet them if possible. It is always possible that you will provide learning and growth opportunities and some of them will leave. You could also ask yourself the question that if you don't provide opportunities for them to learn and grow and they stay, do you really want them? The days of long-term, loyal employees are gone. The people coming in to the workforce today may have watched their parents be rewarded for loyalty by being laid off or having their jobs eliminated. These young people are also generally better educated and skilled than the workforce of the past, and they also are managing their own careers instead of letting you do it.

Technology is becoming such a differentiator in many ways, and most of the young people you want to hire have strong technology skills. You may as well accept that the nature of the workforce has changed, but human behavior has not changed much at the core. All the things we have talked about in the **seven steps** still apply. Even though the new workforce may not be as loyal as the workforce of the past, they have the potential to be very engaged and productive while they are on your team. You can have a big impact on whether they are engaged and productive or not, as well as how long they stay.

We have nearly reached the end of our short journey. I hope you have enjoyed the trip and picked up a few ideas that you can use. My objective will have been met if you find yourself keeping this book handy and occasionally referring to it when you are having challenges achieving the full engagement of your workforce. However you do it, the time you spend working on the **seven steps** and applying them will produce positive results and in the process, you will feel good about your efforts.

Now the last bits and pieces for you

In closing I want to leave you with a short story and a tool you can use. While I was in the Coaching Certification Program at Georgetown University I was introduced to the practice of using a journal. When this was first mentioned in class, I had a vision of a white vinyl diary, with a lock, that some young girl might use to record romantic thoughts and then hide it in the bottom of a drawer. My immediate conclusion was "no way I'm going to use a diary or journal or whatever it might be called." Very open minded of me, don't you think?

I soon found out that to successfully complete the requirements to graduate from the coaching program, I was going to have to use a journal. They had designed the program so that journaling became a key part of the process, and there was no way around it. I finally resigned myself to the fact that I was going to have to learn to use a journal.

The only way I could get my head around using a journal was to go buy a very nice, expensive MANLY journal (you can actually do that), get a special pen, and make journaling a special event, a sort of ceremony.

I bought the great journal and pen and began to use the journal. Once I managed to begin thinking correctly about what the journal was designed to accomplish and started using it, without viewing the process as a myopic jerk, I noticed an amazing thing. Using the journal actually became valuable and I even began to enjoy it, a little.

The tool I leave you with is the journal and the process of journaling. If you don't have a journal, I suggest that you go purchase one. You can find a great selection at your local bookstore, stationary store, Staples or other office supply store and many places online. Wherever you go, just go buy one. I am not going to give you instructions on how to use the journal. I will only tell you how I use mine.

I use my journal when I am struggling with one of those decisions that can have a major impact on my life, or when I want to change a behavior and can't seem to get to it. I'm not suggesting that this is the only thing a journal is good for, but I find it particularly helpful in these situations. You may also find that using it daily to record all the things you are grateful for will support your ability to stay positive even in times of challenge.

The benefit I get from using my journal is that it takes my thoughts that are spinning around in my head, gets them out of the head noise, and makes them real when I can see them on paper. When I can see a situation, challenge, decision, or whatever, come out of my head and on to a piece of paper, written by me, it provides instant clarity. It helps me to be able to step back from the situation and look at it as if I was watching someone else struggle with whatever the issue is.

You may find that using a journal has different benefits for you, but you will find it beneficial, if you think about it in the right way.

Buy a journal, make it special, use it and enjoy it.

References and Resources

The books and other resources listed below are provided for your further research and learning.

Leadership

Leaders—Bennis and Nanus

Principle Centered Leadership—Covey

Servant Leadership—Greenleaf

The Feiner Points of Leadership—Feiner

Secrets of the Wild Goose—Weiss

Leader to Leader—Hesselbein and Cohen

The Corporate Mystic—Hendricks and Ludeman

Primal Leadership—Goleman, Boyatzis and McKee

The Situational Leader—Hersey

Good to Great—Collins

Leadership from the Inside out—Cashman

The Leadership Challenge—Kozes and Posner

Drucker (a special category)

Managing in a Time of Great Change

The Essential Drucker

The Daily Drucker

Behavioral Standbys

Maslow on Management—Maslow

The Motivation to work—Herzberg (out of print)

The Human Side of Enterprise—McGregor

The Management of Organizational Behavior—Hersey and Blanchard

Human Motivation—McClelland

Recognition, Rewards, Engagement and Focus

The Great Game of Business—Jack Stack

A Stake in the Outcome—Jack Stack

Follow This Path—Coffman and Gonzales

The Power of Full Engagement—Loehr and Schwartz

How Full is Your Bucket?—Rath and Clifton

The Goal—Goldratt

A Goal is a Dream with a Deadline—Helzel

Fun at Work—Weinstein

Joy at Work—Bakke

Fun is Good—Veeck and Williams

The Balanced Scorecard—Kaplan and Norton

Successful Management by Objectives—Albrecht

The Enthusiastic Employee—Sirota, Mischkind and Meltzed

The Seven Reasons Employees Leave—Branham

The Engagement Equation—Rice, Marlow and Masarech

Employee Engagement—Macey, Schneider, Barbera and Young

Miscellaneous, Worth Your Time

The Art of Possibility—Zander and Zander

How the Way We Talk Can Change the Way We Work—Kegan and Lahey

Blink—Malcom Gladwell

Immunity to Change—Kegan and Lahey

Creating We—Glaser

Then Wisdom of Teams—Katzenbach and Smith

Mastering Strategy—Grigsby and Greco

Start Where You Are—Rouse

The Little Red Book of Selling....Jeffrey Gitomer

The Strategy Focused Organization—Kaplan and Norton

Living Strategy—Gratton

Focus—Daniel Goleman

Drive—Daniel Pink

Flourish—Martin Seligman

The Progress Principle—Amabile and Kramer

Charlie Martin

Biography

Charlie Martin is founder and head coach of Think Change, where he focuses on workforce engagement, performance management and executive coaching.

He is an executive leadership coach with over 12 years of coaching experience and an experienced senior operating executive with over 35 years of successful experience leading, coaching and developing teams to achieve results. He has led employee groups as large as 8,000 dispersed globally to a few located locally. He has held CEO, COO, EVP, Sr. VP and VP positions in a variety of industries and functions.

Charlie holds an M.A. and B.S. from the University of Central Missouri, is certified as an Executive Leadership Coach by Georgetown University (2002) and is certified as a Professional Certified Coach (PCC) by the International Coach Federation (ICF). He is a trained facilitator of "Immunity to Change."

Subscribe to his blog at www.fromoktoexcellence.com.

Charlie can also be reached at charlie@thinkchange.co or 214-869-6148.

www.linkedin/in/thinkchangeco

www.thinkchange.co

Made in the USA
San Bernardino, CA
10 April 2017